D1569990

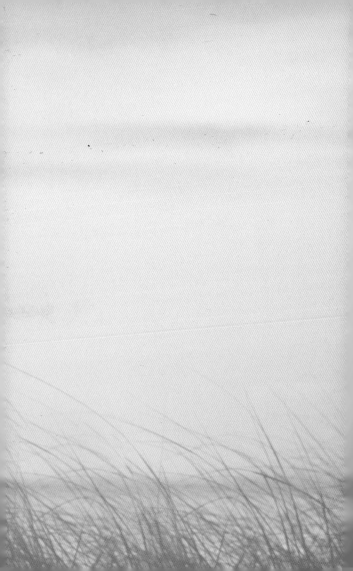

To:

From:

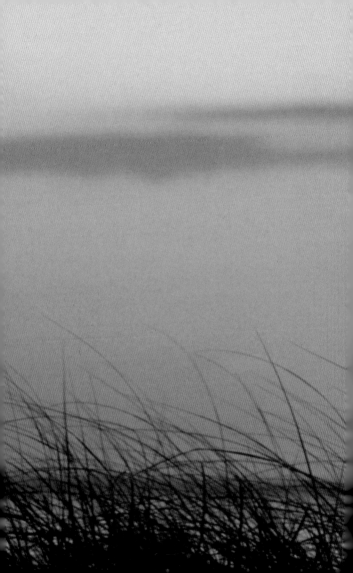

365 Devotions to Inspire Your Day

hugs™

Daily Inspirations

Words of Comfort

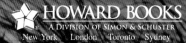

HOWARD BOOKS
A DIVISION OF SIMON & SCHUSTER
New York London Toronto Sydney

Our purpose at Howard Books is to:

• *Increase faith* in the hearts of growing Christians

• *Inspire holiness* in the lives of believers

• *Instill hope* in the hearts of struggling people everywhere

Because He's coming again!

Published by Howard Books, a division of Simon & Schuster, Inc.
1230 Avenue of the Americas, New York, NY 10020
www.howardpublishing.com

Library of Congress Cataloging-in-Publication Data
Hugs daily inspirations words of comfort : 365 devotions to inspire your day / [compiled by Criswell Freeman].
p. cm.
1. Devotional calendars. I. Freeman, Criswell. II. Title.
BV4810.F694 2007
242'.2–dc22

2007023434

ISBN-13: 978-1-4165-4181-3
ISBN-10: 1-4165-4181-0

11 10 9 8 7 6 5 4 3 2

HOWARD and colophon are registered trademarks of Simon & Schuster, Inc.

Manufactured in China

For information regarding special discounts for bulk purchases, please contact Simon & Schuster Special Sales at 1-800-456-6798 or business@simonandschuster.com.

Compiled by Criswell Freeman
Edited by Between the Lines
Cover design by Stephanie D. Walker
Interior design by Bart Dawson

There is a place of quiet rest,
there is a place of comfort sweet,
near to the heart of God.

—Cleland B. McAfee

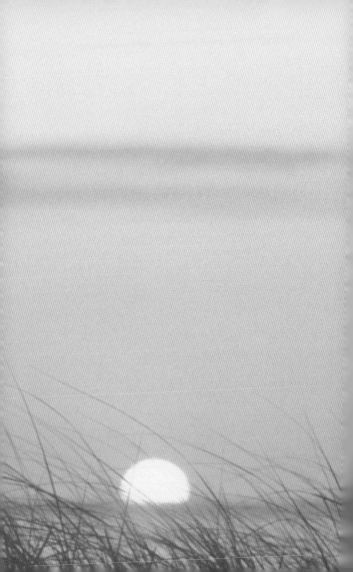

Introduction

Comfort. It's an easy thing to define, but it can be a difficult thing to find, especially in our troubled world. All around us we see challenges—some great and some small. And we have obligations that at times threaten to overwhelm us. So where can we turn to find comfort? To God, of course. And this book can help.

This book contains 365 devotional readings intended to help you find comfort in the everyday corners of your life—comfort at home, comfort at work, comfort at church, comfort at play, and comfort everyplace in between. This book is also intended to make you smile and to make you think. It contains inspirational Bible verses, thought-provoking quotations, and brief essays—all of which can lift your spirits and guide your path.

So today, as you embark upon the next step of your life's journey—a journey that can and should be a cause for celebration—give yourself an emotional hug by thinking of ways you can find—and keep—God's blessings. And while you're searching for the peace God has promised, be quick to share it too. When you do, you'll discover that comfort is like honey: It's hard to spread it around without getting some on yourself.

January

Finding Comfort in an Uncomfortable World

Peace I leave with you; My peace I give to you;
not as the world gives do I give to you.
Do not let your heart be troubled, nor let it be fearful.
John 14:27 NASB

Sometimes the world can be an uncomfortable place. We may find ourselves rushing from point A to point Z with scarcely a moment to spare, all the while being bombarded by news that seems to signify imminent doom. How, then, can we find the assurance and comfort we so earnestly desire? By relying on God.

Today you are beginning a year of personal and spiritual growth. So as a gift to yourself, to your family, and to your friends, promise that you will do all within your power to seek and maintain the inner peace God gives. It is offered freely; it has been paid for in full; it is yours for the asking. So ask. And then share.

True contentment is a thing as active as agriculture.
It is the power of getting out of any situation
all there is in it.
G. K. Chesterton

Faith Is the Answer

This is the victory that has overcome the world—our faith.

1 John 5:4 NKJV

Do you desire the comfort, abundance, and victory God has promised? If so, you'll need to build a life that's founded upon faith: faith in your Creator, faith in yourself, faith in your family, and faith in the future. But sometimes finding and keeping faith can be difficult . . . and that's where God comes in.

If you place your life and your future in God's hands, your faith will most certainly be rewarded. But if you try to rely solely upon your own resources—if you seek to fly solo, without the assurance of your heavenly Father or the assistance of your loved ones—you're heading for trouble, and fast.

So today, make sure you do whatever is required to build your life upon a firm foundation of faith. Then, when you've entrusted your future to the Giver of all things good, rest assured that your future is secure, not only for today, but for all eternity.

Faith is the quiet place within us where we don't get whiplash every time life tosses us a curve.

Patsy Clairmont

An Attitude of Gratitude

Whatever is true, whatever is honorable,
whatever is just, whatever is pure, whatever is lovely,
whatever is commendable . . . dwell on these things.
Philippians 4:8 HCSB

How will you direct your thoughts today? Will you follow the advice in Philippians 4:8 by dwelling on what is honorable, just, and commendable? Or will you let your thoughts be hijacked by the negativity that seems to dominate our troubled world? Are you fearful, angry, bored, or worried? Are you so preoccupied with the concerns of this day that you fail to thank God for the promise of eternity? Are you confused, bitter, or pessimistic? If so, God wants you to know He has better plans for you.

God wants you to experience joy and abundance. So today, and every day hereafter, celebrate the life God has given you by focusing your thoughts on those things that are worthy of praise. Today, count your blessings instead of your hardships. And thank the Giver of all good things for His gifts, which are too numerous to count.

The mind is like a clock that is constantly running down.
It has to be wound up daily with good thoughts.
Fulton J. Sheen

Asking for Directions

If you need wisdom, ask our generous God,
and he will give it to you. He will not
rebuke you for asking.

James 1:5 NLT

Genuine, heartfelt prayer produces powerful changes in us and in our world. When we lift our hearts to God, we open ourselves to a never-ending source of divine wisdom and infinite love. Jesus made it clear to His disciples: they should petition God to meet their needs. So should we.

Do you have questions about your future that you simply can't answer? Do you have needs that you can't meet by yourself? Do you sincerely seek to know God's plan for your life? If so, ask Him for direction, for protection, and for strength—and then keep asking Him every day that you live. Whatever your need, no matter how great or small, pray about it and have faith. God is not just near; He is here, and He's perfectly capable of answering your prayers. It's up to you to ask.

You need not cry very loud;
He is nearer to us than we think.

Brother Lawrence

God Wants to Use You

To everything there is a season,
a time for every purpose under heaven.
Ecclesiastes 3:1 NKJV

Each morning, as the sun rises in the east, you welcome a new day—one that is filled to the brim with opportunities, with possibilities, and with God. As you contemplate God's blessings in your own life, prayerfully seek His guidance for the day ahead.

Discovering God's unfolding purpose for your life is a daily journey, a pilgrimage guided by the teachings of God's holy Word. As you reflect upon His promises and upon the meaning those promises hold for you, ask God to lead you throughout the coming day. Let your heavenly Father direct your steps; concentrate on what God wants you to do now, and leave the distant future in hands that are far more capable than your own: His hands.

We aren't just thrown on this earth like
dice tossed across a table.
We are lovingly placed here for a purpose.
Charles Swindoll

This Is the Day

I have spoken these things to you so that
My joy may be in you and your joy may be complete.
John 15:11 HCSB

God gives us this day; He fills it with possibilities, and He challenges us to use it for His purposes. Psalm 118 reminds us that today, like every other day, is cause for celebration. This day is presented to us fresh and clean, free of charge, but we must remember that today is a nonrenewable resource—once it's gone, it's gone forever. Our responsibility is to use this day in the service of God and according to His will.

Treasure this day God has given you. Give Him the glory and the praise and the thanksgiving He deserves. And search for the hidden possibilities God has placed along your path. Today is a priceless gift from God, so use it joyfully, and encourage others to do the same. After all, this is the day the Lord has made. Rejoice and be glad in it!

All our life is a celebration for us; we are convinced, in
fact, that God is always everywhere.
We sing while we work . . . we pray
while we carry out all life's other occupations.
Saint Clement of Alexandria

Your Highest Aspirations

You are my hope; O Lord God, You are my confidence.

Psalm 71:5 NASB

Are you willing to think big, to dream big, and to pray big? Are you willing to ask God to move mountains in your life, not just molehills? Are you an optimistic person who firmly believes that God is in control and that He protects people (like you) who honor and obey Him? If so, you are wise, and you are blessed.

Some folks seem determined to keep their expectations in check, fearing that things won't work out and their hopes will be dashed. But when we choose not to expect the best from life—when we're too fearful or too pessimistic to hope for the best—we try to superimpose limitations on a God who has none.

So today and every day hereafter, focus on your highest aspirations, and trust that God can help you achieve them . . . because He can.

Faith ought not to be a plaything.
If we believe, we should believe like giants.

Mary McLeod Bethune

The Power of Prayer

The intense prayer of the righteous is very powerful.
James 5:16 HCSB

The power of prayer: these words are familiar, yet sometimes we forget what they mean. Prayer helps us find strength for today and hope for the future. Prayer is not a thing to be taken lightly or to be used infrequently. It is a powerful tool for communicating with our Creator, an opportunity to commune with the Giver of all good gifts.

The quality of your spiritual life will be in direct proportion to the quality of your prayer life. So today, instead of turning things over in your mind, turn them over to God in prayer. Instead of worrying about your next decision, ask God to lead the way. Pray constantly about things great and small. God is always listening, and He wants to hear from you now.

Where there is much prayer,
there will be much of the Spirit;
where there is much of the Spirit,
there will be ever-increasing power.
Andrew Murray

Measuring Your Words

From a wise mind comes wise speech;
the words of the wise are persuasive.
Proverbs 16:23 NLT

If you seek to be a source of encouragement to friends, to family members, and to coworkers, you know you must measure your words carefully. And that's exactly what God wants you to do. His Word reminds us again and again that kind words bring comfort to those who hear them.

Today, make this promise to yourself: Vow to be an honest, effective, encouraging communicator at work, at home, and everyplace in between. Speak wisely, not impulsively. Use words of praise, not words of anger or derision. Learn how to be truthful without being cruel. Remember that you have the power to heal others or to injure them, to lift others up or to bring them down. And when you learn how to lift them up, you'll soon discover that you've lifted yourself up too.

When someone does something good, applaud!
You will make two people happy.
Sam Goldwyn

The Fear Factor

Jesus immediately said to them:
"Take courage! It is I. Don't be afraid."
Matthew 14:27 NIV

A storm rose quickly on the Sea of Galilee, and Jesus's disciples were afraid. Although they had seen Jesus perform many miracles, they feared for their lives, so they turned to their Master—and He calmed the waters and the wind.

Sometimes we, like the disciples, feel threatened by the inevitable storms of life. And when we're fearful, we, too, can turn to the Master for courage and for comfort. The next time you're afraid, remember that the One who calmed the wind and the waves will calm the storms in your own life if you let Him. And remember that the ultimate battle has already been won at Calvary. When you place your trust in God's promises, you can live courageously.

Courage is fear that has said its prayers.
Dorothy Bernard

Not Enough Hours?

It is good to give thanks to the Lord,
to sing praises to the Most High.
It is good to proclaim your unfailing love in the morning
your faithfulness in the evening.
Psalm 92:1–2 NLT

If you ever find that you're simply "too busy" for a daily chat with your Father in heaven, it's time to take a long, hard look at your priorities and your values. Each day has 1,440 minutes—do you value your relationship with God enough to spend a few of those minutes with Him? He deserves that much of your time and more—is He receiving it from you? Hopefully so.

As you consider your plans for the day ahead, organize your life around this simple principle: God first. When you place your Creator where He belongs—at the center of your day and your life—the rest of your priorities will fall into place.

God calls us to seek Him daily
in order to serve Him daily.
Sheila Cragg

God's Guidance

The Lord directs the steps of the godly.
He delights in every detail of their lives.
Psalm 37:23 NLT

God is intensely interested in your life, your faith, and your future. And He will guide your steps if you let Him. When you sincerely offer heartfelt prayers to your heavenly Father, He will give direction and meaning to your life. If you humbly seek His will, He will touch your heart and lead you on the path of His choosing.

Will you trust God to guide your steps? When you entrust your life to Him completely and without reservation, God will give you the strength to meet any challenge, the courage to face any trial, and the wisdom to live in His righteousness and in His peace. So trust Him today and seek His guidance. When you do, you can take each step with faith and confidence.

A spiritual discipline is necessary in order to move slowly from an absurd to an obedient life, from a life filled with noisy worries to a life in which there is some free inner space where we can listen to our God and follow His guidance.
Henri Nouwen

Limitless Power, Limitless Love

I pray also that you will . . . know that God's power is very great for us who believe.

Ephesians 1:18–19 NCV

Because God's power is limitless, it is far beyond the comprehension of mortal minds. Yet even though we cannot fully understand the awesome power of God, we can praise Him for it. When we worship God with faith and assurance, when we place Him at the absolute center of our lives, we invite His love into our hearts. In turn, we grow to love Him more deeply as we sense His love for us. St. Augustine wrote, "I love You, Lord, not doubtingly, but with absolute certainty. Your Word beat upon my heart until I fell in love with You, and now the universe and everything in it tells me to love You."

Let us pray that we, too, will turn our hearts to the Creator, knowing with certainty that His heart has ample room for each of us and that we, in turn, must make room in our hearts for Him.

Our ways may seem good to us. We may even enjoy some moderate successes. But when we do the work of God in our own ways, we will never see the power of God in what we do. God reveals His ways because that is the only way to accomplish His purposes.

Henry Blackaby

When Opportunity Knocks

Whatever you do, work at it with all your heart,
as working for the Lord, not for men.
Colossians 3:23 NIV

The year was 1963, and the woman was in her mid-forties. She took her life savings, started her own business, and began selling cosmetics the hard way—door-to-door, one customer at a time.

Today her company ranks among the leaders in the cosmetics industry. She was able to achieve that level of business success because of her ability to enlist the enthusiastic support of an energetic sales force.

Her name? Mary Kay Ash. She once observed, "A mediocre idea that generates enthusiasm will go farther than a great idea that inspires no one."

Take that tip from Mary Kay, and the next time opportunity knocks on your door, open it with enthusiasm. Excitement is contagious. But if you want to change the world, the first person you must inspire is yourself.

Man's mind is not a container to be filled
but rather a fire to be kindled.
Dorothea Brande

Look Up and Move On

Let all bitterness, wrath, anger, clamor, and evil speaking be put away from you, with all malice. And be kind to one another, tenderhearted, forgiving one another, even as God in Christ forgave you.

Ephesians 4:31–32 NKJV

The world holds few, if any, rewards for those who remain angrily focused on the past. Still, the act of forgiveness is difficult for even the most saintly men and women. Are you mired in the quicksand of bitterness or resentment? If so, it's time for a thorough mental bath, starting today.

Being frail, fallible, imperfect human beings, most of us are quick to anger, quick to blame, slow to forgive, and even slower to forget. Yet the Bible teaches us to forgive others just as we have been forgiven.

If you hold bitter feelings toward even one person—alive or dead—it's time to forgive. Or perhaps you're harboring regret for some past mistake or shortcoming. If so, it's time to forgive yourself and move on. Hatred, bitterness, and regret are not part of God's plan for your life. Forgiveness is.

Life appears to me too short to be spent in nursing animosity, or registering wrongs.

Charlotte Brontë

Finding Comfort Every Day

Peace, peace to you, and peace to your helpers!
For your God helps you.
1 Chronicles 12:18 NKJV

In the world of advertising, comfort is a popular word. Marketers extol the value of comfortable clothes, comfortable shoes, comfortable furniture, comfortable automobiles, even "comfort" foods. But despite advertisers' claims to the contrary, genuine comfort, the kind of inner peace and contentment we all desire, can't be purchased at a store. Lasting comfort begins in the heart . . . and comes from God.

Where do you go to find comfort? Are you seeking the kind of comfort the world promises but so often fails to deliver? Or are you seeking the inner peace and comfort that flows from the loving Creator of the universe?

Seek God each day. When you do, He will comfort you every day.

When I am criticized, injured, or afraid,
there is a Father who is ready to comfort me.
Max Lucado

Finding Comfort in God's Promises

Let's keep a firm grip on the promises that keep us going. He always keeps his word.

Hebrews 10:23 MSG

The Christian faith is founded upon promises that are contained in a unique book. That book is the Bible. The Bible is a road map for life here on earth and for life eternal. We are called upon to study its meaning, to trust its promises, to follow its instructions, and to share its good news. God's Word is a transforming, life-changing, one-of-a-kind treasure. A mere passing acquaintance with the Good Book is insufficient for those who seek to understand God and discern His will.

God has made promises to you, and He intends to keep them. So take Him at His Word. Trust His promises, and share them with your family, with your friends, and with the world. Why not start today?

We can have full confidence in God's promises because we can have full faith in His character.

Franklin Graham

The Cure for Guilt

If you hide your sins, you will not succeed.
If you confess and reject them, you will receive mercy.
Proverbs 28:13 NCV

All of us have made mistakes, and all of us have, at times, displeased God. Sometimes our sins have resulted from our own stubborn rebellion against God's commandments. And sometimes we've been swept up in events around us, leading us to make poor choices. Under either set of circumstances, we may experience feelings of guilt. But God has an answer for the condemnation we feel. That answer is His grace. When we ask God for forgiveness, He gives it. Period.

Are you troubled by feelings of guilt or regret? If so, ask God to forgive you. Take stock of your actions and stop doing the things you're not proud of. Finally, forgive yourself just as God has forgiven you—thoroughly, unconditionally . . . and immediately.

There is nothing, absolutely nothing,
that God will not forgive.
You cannot "out-sin" His forgiveness.
You cannot "out-sin" the love of God.
Kathy Troccoli

Finding Happiness

Happy is the one . . . whose hope is in the Lord.
Psalm 146:5 HCSB

Happiness depends less on our circumstances than on our mind-set. When we turn our thoughts to things positive–when we thank God for His gifts and revel in His glorious creations–we'll reap the rewards of those positive meditations. But when we focus on the negative aspects of life, we invite needless suffering into our lives and, by extension, the lives of our loved ones.

The Roman poet Horace said, "You traverse the world in search of happiness, which is within the reach of every man. A contented mind confers it on all." These words remind us that happiness is, to a surprising extent, up to us.

Here are two facts worth considering: God wants you to know true joy, but you must choose to accept the joy He offers. The way to do that is to meditate on and put your hope in Him. Today, direct your thoughts accordingly and you'll be looking in the right place for true happiness.

Happiness doesn't depend upon who you are or what you have; it depends upon what you think.
Dale Carnegie

Sharing the Gift of Hope

May He grant you according to your heart's desire,
and fulfill all your purpose.
Psalm 20:4 NKJV

One way we can give comfort to our loved ones is by sharing words of encouragement and hope. Hope, like so many human emotions, is contagious.

When we associate with optimistic family members and friends, we are encouraged by their faith and buoyed by their optimism. But discouragement is contagious too, and if we spend too much time in the company of pessimists, our attitudes, like theirs, will tend to be cynical and negative.

So today, look for reasons to celebrate God's endless blessings. And while you're at it, look for people who will join you in the celebration. You'll be better for their company, and they'll be better for yours.

People who inspire others are those
who see invisible bridges at the end
of dead-end streets.
Charles Swindoll

Infinite Possibilities

Is any thing too hard for the Lord?
Genesis 18:14 KJV

Are you afraid to ask God to work miracles in your life? If so, it's time to abandon your doubts and to reclaim your faith in God's promises.

Our Creator is a God of infinite possibilities. But sometimes, because of limited faith and incomplete understanding, we wrongly assume that God cannot or will not intervene in the affairs of mankind. But that's simply not true.

God's Word makes it clear that absolutely nothing is impossible for the Lord. And since the Bible means what it says, you can be comforted in the knowledge that the Creator of the universe can do miraculous things in your life and in the lives of your loved ones. Your task is simple: to take God at His Word . . . and expect the miraculous.

God specializes in things thought impossible.
Catherine Marshall

Relying on God

Humble yourselves under the mighty hand of God,
that He may exalt you at the proper time,
casting all your anxiety on Him, because He cares for you.
1 Peter 5:6–7 NASB

Do the demands of this day threaten to overwhelm you? If so, take heart—and remember to rely not only on your own resources or on your family and friends, but also on the promises of your Father in heaven.

God is a never-ending source of support and courage for those who call on Him. When we are weary, He gives us strength. When we see no hope, God reminds us of His promises. When we grieve, God comforts us.

God will hold your hand and walk with you every day of your life if you let Him. So even when your circumstances are difficult, trust the Father. His love is eternal, and His goodness endures forever.

Faith is not merely you holding on to God—
it is God holding on to you.
E. Stanley Jones

Growing with God

When I was a child, I spoke as a child,
I understood as a child, I thought as a child;
but when I became a man, I put away childish things.
1 Corinthians 13:11 NKJV

Norman Vincent Peale had the following advice for believers of all ages: "Ask the God who made you to keep remaking you." That advice is perfectly sound but often ignored.

The journey toward spiritual and emotional maturity lasts a lifetime. As responsible adults, we can and should continue to grow as long as we live.

When we cease to grow, either emotionally or spiritually, we do ourselves a profound disservice. But if we behave responsibly, if we surround ourselves with encouraging people, and if we do our best to stay in the center of God's will, we won't become stagnant. We'll keep growing . . . and that's exactly what God wants us to do.

People should not worry as much
about what they do but rather about what they are.
If they and their ways are good,
then their deeds are radiant.
Meister Eckhart

Honoring God

Honor God with everything you own;
give him the first and the best.
Your barns will burst, your wine vats will brim over.
Proverbs 3:9 MSG

At times, your life is probably hectic, challenging, and complicated. When the demands of life leave you rushing from place to place with scarcely a moment to spare, it's easy to forget to pause and thank your Creator for the blessings He has bestowed on you. It's easy, but it's also a big mistake.

Whom will you choose to honor today? If you honor God and place Him at the center of your life, every day is a cause for celebration.

Honor God for who He is and for what He has done for you. And don't just honor Him on Sunday morning. Praise Him all day, every day, for as long as you live . . . and then for all eternity.

God shows unbridled delight when He sees people acting in ways that honor Him.
Bill Hybels

Live Your Life

What a gift life is to those who stay the course! You've heard, of course, of Job's staying power, and you know how God brought it all together for him at the end. That's because God cares, cares right down to the last detail.

James 5:11 MSG

She was raised in a one-room cabin with eleven brothers and sisters near the tiny Tennessee hamlet of Locust Ridge. From those humble beginnings emerged the one and only Dolly Parton.

Today, Dolly's songs have become classics, her image is recognizable the world over, and her business empire is enormous. Yet she still lives by a simple, homespun philosophy that never fails. Dolly says, "Nobody's gonna live for you."

If your dreams haven't yet come true, try this: instead of waiting for your big break, start working for it. And get busy now. Because it's your life, and the living is up to you.

Our attitude towards others determines their attitude towards us.

Earl Nightingale

Forgiving and Forgetting

Real wisdom, God's wisdom, begins with a holy life and is characterized by getting along with others. It is gentle and reasonable, overflowing with mercy and blessings.

James 3:17 MSG

Most of us find it difficult to forgive the people who have hurt us. And that's too bad, because life would be much simpler and more pleasant if we could forgive people "once and for all" and be done with it. But forgiveness is seldom that easy. Usually the decision to forgive is straightforward; it's the process of forgiving that's more difficult. Forgiveness is a journey that requires time, perseverance, and prayer.

If you sincerely wish to forgive someone, pray for that person–and keep praying. While you're at it, pray for yourself too, asking God to heal your heart. Don't expect forgiveness to be easy or instantaneous, but rest assured that with God as your partner, you can forgive and enjoy a life of peace with those around you.

In this life, if you have anything to pardon, pardon quickly. Slow forgiveness is little better than no forgiveness.

Arthur Wing Pinero

Learning from Mistakes

I waited patiently for the Lord; he turned to me and heard my cry. He lifted me out of the slimy pit, out of the mud and mire; he set my feet on a rock and gave me a firm place to stand. He put a new song in my mouth, a hymn of praise to our God.

Psalm 40:1–3 NIV

Life can be a struggle at times. And everybody (including you) makes mistakes. But our goal should be to make them only once.

Have you experienced a recent setback? If so, look for the lesson God is trying to teach you. Instead of complaining about life's sad state of affairs, learn what needs to be learned, change what needs to be changed, and move on. View failure as an opportunity to realign your life with God's will. View disappointment as opportunities to learn more about yourself and your world.

The next time you make one of life's inevitable blunders, choose to turn your misstep into a stepping-stone. Then step right past failure to success.

Mistakes are part of the dues one pays for a full life.

Sophia Loren

Finding Comfort Outside Your Comfort Zone

The Lord is my light and my salvation; whom shall I fear?
The Lord is the strength of my life;
of whom shall I be afraid?
Psalm 27:1 NKJV

Have you spent too much time playing it safe? Are you uncomfortably stuck inside your comfort zone? Would you like to change the quality and direction of your life, but you're not sure how? If you answered these questions in the affirmative, maybe you're more afraid of change than you need to be.

Change is often difficult and sometimes uncomfortable. But the world keeps changing, and the longer you delay needed changes, the more painful they'll become. Instead of fighting change, maybe it's time to embrace it.

The next time you face a decision that involves a major modification in your own circumstances, look to God. He will give you the courage to step outside your comfort zone.

You gain strength, courage, and confidence by every experience in which you really stop to look fear in the face. You are able to say to yourself, "I lived through this horror. I can take the next thing that comes along." You must do the things you think you cannot do.
Eleanor Roosevelt

Thanksgiving, Yes . . . Envy, No!

A heart at peace gives life to the body,
but envy rots the bones.
Psalm 14:30 NIV

As the recipient of God's grace, you have every reason to celebrate life. After all, God has promised you the opportunity to receive His abundance and His joy—in fact, you have the opportunity to receive those gifts right now. But if you allow envy to gnaw away at the fabric of your soul, you'll find that joy remains elusive. When you're envious of others, you unintentionally rob yourself of the comfort and peace that might otherwise be yours.

So do yourself an enormous favor: rather than succumbing to envy, focus on the marvelous things God has done for you. Thank the Giver of all good gifts, and keep thanking Him for the wonders of His love and the miracles of His creation. Count your own blessings, and let your neighbors count theirs. It's a happier way to live.

You can't be envious and happy at the same time.
Frank Tyger

Your Unique Gifts

God has given each of you a gift from his great variety of spiritual gifts. Use them well to serve one another.

1 Peter 4:10 NLT

The old saying is both familiar and true: "What we are is God's gift to us; what we become is our gift to God." Each of us possesses special talents, given to us by God, that can be nurtured or ignored. Our challenge is to use those abilities to the greatest extent possible—and to use them in ways that honor our Creator.

Are you using your talents to make the world a better place? If so, keep up the good work! But perhaps you have gifts that you haven't fully explored and developed. Why not have a chat today with the One who gave you those gifts? Your talents are priceless treasures bestowed on you by your heavenly Father. Use them. After all, the best way to say thank you to the Giver is to use what He has given.

God has given you special talents—now it's your turn to give them back to God.

Marie T. Freeman

Where Is God Leading?

When troubles come your way, consider it an opportunity for great joy. For . . . when your faith is tested, your endurance has a chance to grow. So let it grow, for when your endurance is fully developed, you will be perfect and complete, needing nothing.

James 1:2–4 NLT

Whether we realize it or not, times of adversity can be times of intense personal and spiritual growth. Our difficult days are also times when we can learn (or relearn) some of life's most important lessons.

The next time you experience a difficult moment, a difficult day, or even a difficult year, ask yourself this question: Where is God leading me? In times of struggle and sorrow, you can take comfort in knowing that God is leading you to a place of His choosing. Your duty is to watch, to pray, to listen, and to follow.

It is only because of problems
that we grow mentally and spiritually.

M. Scott Peck

February

No Need to Worry

Trust in him at all times, O people;
pour out your hearts to him, for God is our refuge.
Psalm 62:8 NIV

In the game of life, you win some and you lose some. Life is risky business; we live in an uncertain world, a world in which trouble may come calling at any moment. No wonder we may find ourselves feeling a little panicky at times.

Do you sometimes spend more time worrying about a problem than you spend solving it? If so, here's a strategy for dealing with your worries: take them to God. Take your troubles to Him; take your fears to Him; take your doubts to Him; take your weaknesses to Him; take your sorrows to Him . . . and leave them all there.

God is the Rock that cannot be moved. When you build your life upon that Rock, you have absolutely no need to worry . . . not now, not ever.

When God is at the center of your life, you worship.
When he's not, you worry.
Rick Warren

God's Guidebook

Every word of God is flawless;
he is a shield to those who take refuge in him.
Proverbs 30:5 NIV

Do you read your Bible a lot . . . or not? The answer to this simple question will determine, to a surprising extent, the quality of your life and of your faith.

As you establish priorities for life, you must choose whether God's Word will be the bright spotlight that guides your path each day or a tiny nightlight that occasionally provides a flicker in the dark. The decision to study the Bible—or not to—is yours and yours alone. But make no mistake: how you choose to use your Bible will have a profound impact on you and your loved ones.

The Bible is the ultimate guide for life; make it your personal guidebook as well. God's message has the power to transform your day . . . and your life.

Reading news without reading the Bible will inevitably lead to an unbalanced life, an anxious spirit, a worried and depressed soul.

Bill Bright

Too Much Busyness, Too Little Peace

Those who love your instructions have great peace and do not stumble.

Psalm 119:165 NLT

Has the hectic pace of life robbed you of the peace that might otherwise be yours? Do you sometimes find yourself overcommitted and underprepared? Are you too busy for your own good? If so, it's probably time to slow down long enough to reorganize your day and reorder your priorities.

God offers every human being (including you) a peace that surpasses mortal understanding; but He doesn't force anyone (including you) to accept it. God's peace is freely offered but not mandated.

Today, as a gift to yourself, to your family, and to the world, be still and experience God's presence. Open your heart to His love. Claim the genuine peace that can be yours for the asking. And then share that blessing and comfort with those around you.

Often our lives are strangled by things that don't ultimately matter.

Grady Nutt

Always with Us

A child is born to us, a son is given to us.
The government will rest on his shoulders.
And he will be called: Wonderful Counselor, Mighty God,
Everlasting Father, Prince of Peace.
Isaiah 9:6 NLT

Are you facing difficult circumstances or unwelcome changes? If so, you can take comfort in knowing that God is far bigger than any problem you may face. So instead of worrying about life's inevitable challenges, put your faith in the Father and His only Son: "Jesus Christ is the same yesterday, today, and forever" (Hebrews 13:8 NKJV). It is precisely because God does not change that you can face your challenges with courage for today and hope for tomorrow.

Life is often trying, but you need not be fearful. God loves you, and He will protect you. In times of hardship, He will comfort you; in times of change, He will guide your steps. When you're troubled or weak or sorrowful, God is always with you. Build your life on the Rock that cannot be moved. Because He's always with you, you can always trust Him.

It is a joy that God never abandons His children.
He guides faithfully all who listen to His directions.
Corrie ten Boom

Quality Time

Teach us to number our days,
that we may gain a heart of wisdom.
Psalm 90:12 NKJV

As you know, caring for your family requires time—lots of time. And you've probably heard about the difference between "quality time" and "quantity time." Your family needs both. So as a responsible member of a loving family, you'll want to invest large quantities of time and energy in the care and nurturing of your clan.

But is your life so busy and your to-do list so full that you scarcely have a moment to spare? Does it seem you can never find quite enough time to spend with your family? If so, today is a good day to begin rearranging your priorities and your life. And while you're at it, make sure God remains squarely at the center of your household. When you do, He will bless you and yours in ways you could have scarcely imagined.

If I were starting my family over again,
I would give first priority to my wife and children, not to my work.
Richard Halverson

Finding Comfort in Church

If two or three people come together in my name,
I am there with them.
Matthew 18:20 NCV

A wonderful place to find comfort is in church. In the book of Acts, Luke reminds us to "be like shepherds to the church of God" (20:28). And what was appropriate in New Testament times is equally true today. We'll be wise to honor God not only in our hearts but also in our houses of worship.

Do you feed your soul by feeding the church of God? Do you attend regularly and are you an active participant? The answer to these questions will have a profound impact on the quality and direction of your spiritual journey.

So do yourself a favor–become actively involved in your church. Don't just go to services out of habit. Join out of a sincere desire to know and worship God. When you do, you'll be blessed by the One who sent His Son to die so that you might have everlasting life.

The church is not an end in itself;
it is a means to the end of the kingdom of God.
E. Stanley Jones

The Voice Inside Your Head

I strive always to keep my conscience clear before God and man.

Acts 24:16 NIV

Your conscience is an early-warning system designed by God to keep you out of trouble. Whenever you're about to make a significant error in judgment, that little voice inside your head has a way of speaking up. If you listen to God as He speaks through your conscience, you'll be wise; if you ignore Him, you'll be putting yourself at risk.

Whenever you're about to make an important decision, listen carefully to God's quiet voice as He whispers in your heart and mind. Sometimes, you would rather drown out that voice and go your own way. From time to time, you'll be tempted to abandon your better judgment. But remember that a conscience is a terrible thing to waste. So instead of ignoring that quiet little voice, pay careful attention to it. Be sure it's tuned in to God's Spirit and in line with His Word. If you do, you'll be led in the right direction. In fact, God wants to lead you right now. Listen to His voice.

Your conscience is your alarm system.
It's your protection.

Charles Stanley

February 8

Listening to God

Listen in silence before me.
Isaiah 41:1 NLT

Sometimes God speaks loudly and clearly. More often, He speaks in a quiet voice—and if you're wise, you'll be listening carefully when He does. To do so, you must carve out quiet moments each day to study His Word and sense His direction.

Can you quiet yourself long enough to listen to your heavenly Father? Are you attuned to the subtle guidance of His Spirit? Are you willing to pray sincerely and then to wait quietly for God's response?

God doesn't usually send His messages on stone tablets or post them on city billboards. He communicates in subtler ways. If you sincerely desire to hear His voice, you must set aside quiet time and create a quiet, willing place in your heart—and listen.

Half an hour of listening is essential
except when one is very busy.
Then, a full hour is needed.
Saint Francis de Sales

No Complaints

*Do everything without complaining or arguing.
Then you will be innocent and without any wrong.*
Philippians 2:14–15 NCV

Most of us have more blessings than we can count, yet we still find reasons to complain about the minor frustrations of everyday life. To do so, of course, is not only shortsighted–it's also a serious roadblock on the path to spiritual abundance.

Would you like to feel more comfortable about your circumstances and your life? Then determine to do whatever it takes to ensure that you focus your thoughts and energy on the major blessings you've received (not the minor inconveniences you must occasionally endure).

The next time you're tempted to gripe about the frustrations of everyday living, don't do it! Today and every day, make it a practice to count your blessings, not your hardships. It's a much more joyful way to live.

*Life is too short to nurse one's misery.
Hurry across the lowlands so that you may spend more time on the mountaintops.*
Phillips Brooks

Beyond Mediocrity

Do not lack diligence; be fervent in spirit; serve the Lord.
Romans 12:11 HCSB

God expects us to conduct ourselves with dignity and discipline. The Bible reminds us again and again that our Creator intends for us to lead disciplined lives—and we should take God at His Word, despite the temptation to take the easy way out.

We live in a world in which leisure is glorified and indifference is often glamorized. But God did not create us for lives of mediocrity; He created us for far greater things.

Life's greatest rewards seldom fall into our laps; to the contrary, our greatest accomplishments usually require lots of work. But God has given us each an adequate measure of strength and ability. He knows we're up to the tasks He sends our way, and He has big plans for us; may we, as disciplined followers of God, always be worthy of those plans.

No horse gets anywhere until he is harnessed . . .
No life ever grows great until it is focused,
dedicated, disciplined.
Harry Emerson Fosdick

Your Marathon Partner

Don't look for shortcuts to God. The market is flooded with surefire, easygoing formulas for a successful life that can be practiced in your spare time. Don't fall for that stuff, even though crowds of people do. The way to life–to God!–is vigorous and requires total attention.

Matthew 7:13–14 MSG

As you seek abundance and peace for your loved ones and yourself, you will undoubtedly also experience your fair share of disappointments, detours, false starts, and failures. When you do, don't become discouraged; God is not finished with you yet.

The old saying is as true today as it was when it was first spoken: "Life is a marathon, not a sprint." That's why wise travelers select a traveling companion who never tires and never falters. That perfect partner is your heavenly Father. So today, as you face the challenges and obligations of everyday life, work as if everything depended upon you, but pray as if everything depended upon God. Then, when you've done your best, you can trust God to do the rest.

We ought to make some progress, however little, every day, and show some increase of fervor. We ought to act as if we were at war–as, indeed, we are–and never relax until we have won the victory.

Saint Teresa of Avila

Imaginary Problems

Jesus said, "Don't let your hearts be troubled.
Trust in God, and trust in me."
John 14:1 NCV

In the golden age of television, Steve Allen shaped the sleeping habits of millions of Americans with his program, *The Tonight Show*. Steve was one of the most versatile and influential entertainers of the twentieth century. But did he ever lose sleep over the many problems associated with live television? Hardly. He said, "One of the nice things about problems is that a good many of them do not exist except in our own imaginations." And he was right.

The next time you find yourself dreading some vaguely defined future event, remember Steve Allen's observation and quit fretting. As Steve indicated, many of our problems are imaginary. And when it comes to facing those that aren't, trusting in God beats worry tonight and every night.

I am an old man and have known
a great many troubles,
but most of them never happened.
Mark Twain

Excellence, Not Excuses

Do you see a man skilled in his work?
He will stand in the presence of kings.
Proverbs 22:29 HCSB

We live in a world where excuses are everywhere. And it's precisely because excuses are numerous that they are also ineffective. When we hear the words, "I'm sorry but . . . ," most of us know exactly what is to follow: the excuse. The dog ate the homework. Traffic was terrible. It's the company's fault. The boss is to blame. The equipment is broken. We're out of that. The list is virtually endless.

Because we humans are so handy with excuses, most of them have been used, reused, overused, and abused. That's why they don't work–we've heard them all before.

So when you're tempted to concoct a new and improved excuse, don't bother. The good ones have all been taken anyway. A far better strategy is this: do the work. And let your excellent performance speak loudly and convincingly for itself.

Replace your excuses with fresh determination.
Charles Swindoll

We're All Role Models

Be an example to the believers
in word, in conduct, in love, in spirit, in faith, in purity.
1 Timothy 4:12 NKJV

Whether we like it or not, all of us are examples. The question is not *whether* we will be examples to our families and friends; the question is *what kind* of examples we'll be.

What kind of example are you? Are you the kind of person whose behavior serves as a positive role model for others? Are you the kind of person whose actions, day in and day out, are based on integrity, fidelity, and self-discipline? If so, you'll be blessed by God—and you'll be a powerful force for good in a world that desperately needs positive influences such as yours.

Live today knowing that others take note of your conduct. Your family and friends are watching . . . and so, for that matter, is God.

Life is not easy for any of us. But it is a continual
challenge, and it is up to us to be cheerful
and to be strong, so that those who depend on us may
draw strength from our example.
Rose Kennedy

Worshipping God Every Day

An hour is coming, and is now here, when the true worshipers will worship the Father in spirit and truth. Yes, the Father wants such people to worship Him. God is Spirit, and those who worship Him must worship in spirit and truth.

John 4:23–24 HCSB

If you genuinely desire to receive God's comfort, you must be willing to worship Him not just on Sunday, but on every day of the week. God has a wonderful plan for your life, and an important part of that plan includes the time you set aside for praise and worship.

Every life, including yours, includes some form of worship. The question is not whether you will worship, but what you worship. If you choose to worship God, you'll reap a bountiful harvest of joy, peace, and abundant blessing. So do yourself and your loved ones this favor: Worship God with sincerity and thanksgiving today and every day. Write His name on your heart—and rest assured that your name is written on His.

If you will not worship God seven days a week, you do not really worship Him even one day a week.

A. W. Tozer

First Place

Fear of the Lord is the foundation of true wisdom.
All who obey his commandments will grow in wisdom.
Psalm 111:10 NLT

If you really want to know God, you can start by putting Him first in your life. So here's a question worth thinking about: have you made God your top priority by offering Him your heart, your soul, your talents, and your time? Or are you in the habit of giving God little more than a few hours on Sunday morning? The answers to these questions will also greatly affect the quality of your life and the content of your character.

Some folks choose to worship God and, as a result, reap the joy He offers to His children. Other folks seem determined to do things their way, with decidedly mixed results. Which kind of person are you? Does God rule your heart? If you sincerely want to know Him, you must answer yes—you must put your Creator in first place.

Attitude is all-important. Let the soul take a quiet attitude of faith and love toward God, and from there on, the responsibility is God's.
He will make good on His commitments.
A. W. Tozer

Richly Blessed

God loves a cheerful giver.
2 Corinthians 9:7 NIV

Are you a cheerful giver? If you follow the instruction in God's Word, you must be. When we give, God looks not only at the quality of our gift but also at the condition of our heart. If we give generously, joyfully, and without complaint, we'll be living in accordance with God's plan. But if we offer our gifts grudgingly, or if our motivation for giving is selfish, our generosity will fall short of pleasing our Creator—even if our gift is a generous one.

Today, pledge to be a cheerful, generous, courageous giver. The world needs your help, and you'll benefit from the spiritual rewards that will be yours when you give faithfully, prayerfully, and cheerfully.

The mind grows by taking in,
but the heart grows by giving out.
Warren Wiersbe

Small Steps Toward Success

Let endurance have its perfect result,
so that you may be perfect and complete,
lacking in nothing.
James 1:4 NASB

In 1886, Anne Sullivan became governess to a young girl named Helen Keller. Helen, who had been left blind and deaf by a childhood illness, was a difficult student at first. But in time, little Helen started learning. Anne became known as "the miracle worker," but she knew that Helen's improvement was actually the result of hard work. Anne observed, "People seldom see the halting and painful steps by which the most insignificant success is achieved."

If you've been impatient for your own success, remember that your giant leap forward will likely be preceded by many little, halting steps. Don't get discouraged. Keep the faith, keep working, and keep putting one foot in front of the other, even if your steps are small ones. After all, every great mountain must be climbed one step at a time.

To tend, unfailingly, unflinchingly,
towards a goal, is the secret of success.
Anna Pavlova

God Is Available

Where can I go from your Spirit? Where can I flee from your presence? If I go up to the heavens, you are there; if I make my bed in the depths, you are there. If I rise on the wings of the dawn, if I settle on the far side of the sea, even there your hand will guide me, your right hand will hold me fast.

Psalm 139:7–10 NIV

If God is everywhere, why does He sometimes seem so far away? The answer to that question really has nothing to do with God; it has to do with us—how we think, how we worship, and how we choose to spend our time.

When we begin each day on our knees, in praise and worship, God often seems near indeed. But if we ignore God's presence or—worse yet—rebel against it altogether, the world in which we live becomes spiritually barren.

Today, and every day, praise God. Wherever you are—whether you're energized or exhausted, happy or sad, victorious or vanquished—celebrate God's presence. Be comforted, for He is here.

There is nothing more important in any life than the constantly enjoyed presence of the Lord. There is nothing more vital, for without it we shall make mistakes, and without it we shall be defeated.

Alan Redpath

His Intimate Love

As the Father loved Me, I also have loved you;
abide in My love.
John 15:9 NKJV

Do you seek an intimate, one-on-one relationship with your heavenly Father, or are you satisfied to keep Him at a "safe" distance? St. Augustine once said, "God loves each of us as if there were only one of us." Do you believe those words?

Even on those difficult days when God seems distant—or even absent—you can be sure that His love for you remains unchanged. He knows every thought, He watches every step, and He hears every prayer. Today and every day, your loving, heavenly Father is waiting patiently for you to reach out to Him. So open your heart to God. You can trust Him and abide in His love without fear and without reservation, because you are His precious child.

God does not love us because we are valuable.
We are valuable because God loves us.
Fulton J. Sheen

Secure in His Hands

Be of good courage, and He shall strengthen your heart, all you who hope in the Lord.
Psalm 31:24 NKJV

Open your Bible to its center, and you'll find the book of Psalms. In it are some of the most beautiful words ever translated into the English language. One of the most beautiful is Psalm 23, in which David describes God as being like a shepherd who cares for His flock. No wonder these verses have provided hope for generations of believers.

You are God's priceless creation, made in His image, and protected by Him. God watches over every step you make and every breath you take, so you need never be afraid.

But fear has a way of slipping into the hearts of even the most faith filled. On occasion, you'll confront circumstances that shake you to the core of your soul. When you're afraid, trust in God. When you're worried, turn your concerns over to Him. When you're anxious, remember the quiet assurance of God's promises. And then place your life in His care. You are secure in His hands.

Entrust yourself entirely to God. He is a Father and a most loving Father at that, who would rather let heaven and earth collapse than abandon anyone who trusted in Him.
Paul of the Cross

Becoming Wise

He who walks with the wise grows wise.

Proverbs 13:20 NIV

Wisdom doesn't spring up overnight—it takes time. To become wise, we must seek God's wisdom and live according to His Word. And we must not only learn the lessons God teaches, but also live by them.

Would you like to experience the comfort and peace that results from a wisely lived life? If so, study the ultimate source of wisdom: the Word of God. Seek out worthy mentors and listen carefully to their advice. Associate, day in and day out, with mature, thoughtful friends. And act in accordance with God's wisdom and guidance gleaned through those resources. When you do these things, you will become wise . . . and you'll be a blessing to your friends, to your family, and to the world.

The process of living seems to consist in coming to realize truths so ancient and simple that, if stated, they sound like barren platitudes. They cannot sound otherwise to those who have not had the relevant experience: that is why there is no real teaching of such truths possible and every generation starts from scratch.

C. S. Lewis

Finding Work You Love

He did it with all his heart. So he prospered.
2 Chronicles 31:21 NKJV

Gracie Allen married George Burns in 1926, and the two formed one of America's most popular comedy teams. Gracie played the role of the confused, linguistically challenged wife, while George played the role of the loving but frustrated husband.

Gracie died in 1964, but George lived until 1996, becoming one of America's most beloved senior citizens. George Burns's "secret of success" was simple: he said, "My best advice is this: fall in love with what you do for a living."

Have you found work that fits your personality and makes the world a better place? If so, you are richly blessed. If not, keep searching—because the world needs your best work, and you should know the joy of finding it.

When you find your passion, not just what you like to do but that which makes you want to get up every morning, you too will have a life-changing experience.
Condoleezza Rice

The Right Kind of Leaders

A good leader plans to do good, and those good things make him a good leader.
Isaiah 32:8 NCV

Our world needs the right kind of leaders—leaders who are willing to honor God with their words and their deeds. But the same is true for your little corner of the world too: your family and friends need people who are willing to lead by example, not merely by proclamation.

If you want to be the right kind of leader, begin by serving as a positive role model to those around you. After all, your words of instruction will never ring true unless you yourself are willing to follow them.

The world needs you, your community needs you, and your family needs you. In fact, since good leaders are a rare treasure, they need you very much. Are you the kind of leader you would want to follow? Make that your goal today.

Leadership is the ability to lift and inspire.
Paul Dietzel

The Wisdom of Moderation

Moderation is better than muscle,
self-control better than political power.
Proverbs 16:32 MSG

Moderation and wisdom are traveling companions. If we are to be wise, we must learn to temper our appetites, our desires, and our impulses. That's not easy, but when we do, we'll be blessed–in part because God has created a world in which temperance is often rewarded and intemperance often punished.

Would you like to improve your life? Then harness your appetites and restrain your impulses. Moderation is difficult, especially in a prosperous society such as ours. But the rewards of moderation are numerous and long lasting. Claim those rewards today. No one can force you to moderate your appetites. The decision to live temperately (and wisely) is yours. But so will be the rewards.

Less is more.
Ludwig Mies van der Rohe

Living on Purpose

In Him we were also made His inheritance, predestined according to the purpose of the One who works out everything in agreement with the decision of His will.

Ephesians 1:11 HCSB

Life is best lived on purpose, not stumbling along by accident. The sooner we discover what God intends for us to do, the better. But God's purposes aren't always clear to us. Sometimes we wander aimlessly in what feels like a wilderness. Or we struggle against God in a vain effort to find success and comfort through our own means rather than according to His plan.

Whenever we struggle against God's plans, we suffer. When we resist God's calling, our efforts bear little fruit. Our best strategy, therefore, is to seek God's wisdom and to follow Him wherever He leads us.

God has a plan for your life. If you seek that plan sincerely and prayerfully, you will find it. When you discover God's purpose for your life, you'll experience abundant blessing, peace, comfort, and power–God's power. And that's the only kind worth having.

Be patient. God is using today's difficulties to strengthen you for tomorrow. He is equipping you. The God who makes things grow will help you bear fruit.

Max Lucado

The Role Our Possessions Should Play

Keep your lives free from the love of money,
and be satisfied with what you have.
Hebrews 13:5 NCV

On the grand stage of a well-lived life, material possessions should play a rather small role. Yet sometimes we allow our possessions to assume undue control over our lives. But God has a better plot for our lives, if we'll allow Him to be the director.

How much of your life are you investing in the pursuit of money and the things money can buy? Do you own your possessions, or are they starting to own more and more of you? Is your life ruled by the quest for riches of an earthly kind or of a spiritual kind?

If material possessions are ruling your life, take careful inventory and rid yourself of the overstock. After all, nothing on earth is valuable enough to allow it to separate you from your Creator. Absolutely nothing.

Theirs is an endless road, a hopeless maze,
who seek for goods before they seek for God.
Saint Bernard of Clairvaux

The Importance of Praise

I will praise You with my whole heart.
Psalm 138:1 NKJV

Life is demanding, and most of us are busy indeed. Sometimes we allow ourselves to become so preoccupied with the demands of daily life that we forget to say thank you to the very One who gives us that life. But the Bible makes it clear, given how often praising God is mentioned, that praise is a vital part of our relationship with God.

Because God is always with us, and because He is always blessing us, worship and praise can—and should—become a part of everything we do. Otherwise, we can quickly lose perspective as we fall prey to the demands of the moment.

Do you sincerely wish to have close fellowship with the One who has given you eternal love and eternal life? Then praise Him today—and every day—for who He is and for all the wonderful things He has done for you.

The Bible instructs—and experience teaches—that praising God results in our burdens being lifted and our joys being multiplied.
Jim Gallery

March

Conquering Everyday Frustrations

A hot-tempered man stirs up dissension,
but a patient man calms a quarrel.
Proverbs 15:18 NIV

Life is full of frustrations, some great and some small.

On occasion you—like Jesus when He confronted the money changers in the temple—will confront evil. When you do, you may respond as He did—vigorously and without reservation.

But more often your frustrations will be of the comparatively mundane variety. As long as you live here on earth, you will face countless opportunities to lose your temper over small, relatively insignificant events: a traffic jam, a spilled cup of coffee, an inconsiderate comment, a broken promise. When you're tempted to lose your temper over the minor inconveniences of life, don't. Turn away from anger, hatred, bitterness, and regret. Turn instead to God and find comfort in Him.

When you strike out in anger,
you may miss the other person,
but you will always hit yourself.
Jim Gallery

Actions That Reflect Our Beliefs

If the way you live isn't consistent with what you believe, then it's wrong.

Romans 14:23 MSG

English clergyman Thomas Fuller observed, "He does not believe who does not live according to his belief." These words are most certainly true. We may proclaim our beliefs to our hearts' content, but our proclamations will mean nothing–to others or to ourselves–unless we accompany our words with matching deeds. The sermons we live are far more compelling than the ones we preach.

Like it or not, your life is an accurate reflection of your creed. If this fact gives you some cause for concern, don't bother talking about the changes you intend to make–make them. Then, when your good deeds speak for themselves–as they most certainly will–the positive message of your life will be clear to all.

There can be no happiness if the things we believe in are different from the things we do.

Freya Stark

A Prescription to Fight Panic

Anxiety in the heart of man causes depression,
but a good word makes it glad.
Proverbs 12:25 NKJV

We live in an uncertain world, a world that sometimes feels like shifting sand beneath our feet. Ours is an anxious society in which the changes we face sometimes threaten to outpace our abilities to adjust. No wonder we occasionally find ourselves beset by feelings of anxiety and panic.

At times, our anxieties may stem from physical causes–chemical imbalances in the brain that result in severe emotional distress. In such cases, modern medicine offers hope to those who suffer. But often our anxieties result from spiritual deficits, not physical ones. And when we're spiritually depleted, the best prescription is found not in the medicine cabinet but deep inside the human heart. What we need is a higher daily dose of God's love, God's peace, God's assurance, and God's presence. And how do we acquire these blessings? Through prayer and meditation, worship, and faith in our Creator.

The thing that preserves a person from panic
is his relationship to God.
Oswald Chambers

Doing the Right Thing

By this we know that we have come to know Him,
if we keep His commandments.
1 John 2:3 NASB

When we behave like thoughtful adults—and when we conduct ourselves in accordance with God's instructions—we'll be blessed in ways we cannot fully anticipate. When we seek righteousness in our own lives—and when we seek the companionship of those who do likewise—we'll reap the spiritual rewards God intends for us to enjoy.

Today, as you fulfill your responsibilities, hold fast to that which is good, and associate with folks who behave in like fashion. When you do, your good works will serve as a powerful example and as a worthy offering to your Creator. And you'll reap a surprising array of blessings as a result.

If you want to be respected for your actions,
then your behavior must be above reproach.
Rosa Parks

You Are Blessed

I will bless them and the places surrounding my hill.
I will send down showers in season;
there will be showers of blessing.
Ezekiel 34:26 NIV

If you sat down and began counting your blessings, how long would it take? Probably a very, very long time! Our blessings include life, freedom, family, friends, talents, and possessions, for starters. But our greatest blessing—a gift that is ours for the asking—is God's gift of salvation through Christ Jesus.

Today, begin making a list of your blessings. You won't be able to make a comprehensive list, but take a few moments and jot down as many blessings as you can. Then give thanks to the Giver of all good things—God. His love for you is eternal, and His gifts are the best kind. And it's never too soon—or too late—to acknowledge those blessings.

God's kindness is not like the sunset—brilliant
in its intensity, but dying every second.
God's generosity keeps coming
and coming and coming.
Bill Hybels

Joy 101

When a man is gloomy, everything seems to go wrong;
when he is cheerful, everything seems right!

Proverbs 15:15 TLB

God promises that we can experience a special kind of abundance and joy. How can we claim these spiritual riches? By trusting God, by obeying His instructions, and by following in the footsteps of His Son, Jesus. When we do these things, God fills our hearts with His power and His love . . . and we experience a peace that surpasses human understanding.

Today, as you go out to meet the many obligations of life, remember to offer praise to your Creator and give thanks for His gifts. As a way of blessing your loved ones and yourself, be quick to share a smile, a kind word, or a hug. And be sure that you're always ready to share God's joy—and His message—with a world that needs both.

When I think of God, my heart is so full of joy that the
notes leap and dance as they leave my pen;
and since God has given me a cheerful heart,
I serve him with a cheerful spirit.

Franz Joseph Haydn

The World . . . and You

Don't copy the behavior and customs of this world,
but let God transform you into a new person
by changing the way you think.
Romans 12:2 NLT

We live in the world, but we must not worship it. Our duty is to place God first and everything else after Him. But because we are fallible beings with imperfect faith, placing God in His rightful place is sometimes difficult. In fact, at almost every turn it seems we are tempted to relegate God to a secondary position in our hearts and minds (or to ignore Him altogether).

Our world is a noisy, distracting place filled with countless opportunities to stray from God's will. The world seems to cry, "Worship me with your time, your money, your energy, and your thoughts!" But God commands otherwise: we are to worship Him first and always. And we won't know the truest happiness until we do.

I have a divided heart, trying to love God and
the world at the same time. God says,
"You can't love me as you should
if you love this world too."
Mary Morrison Suggs

The Importance of Prayer

*Rejoice evermore. Pray without ceasing.
In every thing give thanks: for this is the will of God in
Christ Jesus concerning you.*
1 Thessalonians 5:16–18 KJV

In his first letter to the Thessalonians, Paul advised his friends to pray without ceasing. That advice is for us today, as well.

Prayer is a powerful tool for communicating with God; it's an opportunity to commune with our heavenly Father. Prayer is not a thing to be taken lightly or to be used infrequently. It is a force for improving our lives, for building our faith, and for improving our world.

Prayer shouldn't be reserved for mealtimes or bedtimes; it should be a steady presence and focus in our daily lives. So today, pray constantly. Talk to God about the big stuff and about the little stuff. He wants to hear from you. God is listening; when you pray, He will answer.

*Nothing is clearer than that prayer has its
only worth and significance in the great fact that God
hears and answers prayer.*
E. M. Bounds

The Morning Watch

Every morning he wakes me. He teaches me to listen like a student. The Lord God helps me learn.
Isaiah 50:4–5 NCV

Each new day is a gift from God, and if we're wise, we'll spend a few quiet moments each morning thanking the Giver.

Warren Wiersbe wrote, "Surrender your mind to the Lord at the beginning of each day." That's sound advice. When you begin each day with your head bowed and your heart lifted, you'll be reminded of God's love, His protection, and His commandments. Then you can align your priorities for the coming day with the teachings in God's Word and the directions He has whispered to your heart.

If you've acquired the unfortunate habit of trying to "squeeze" God into the corners of your life, it's time to reshuffle the items on your to-do list and place God first—in your life and in your day. If you haven't already done so, form the habit of spending quality time with your Father in heaven. You'll find it makes all the difference.

Are you weak? Weary? Confused? Troubled? Pressured? How is your relationship with God? Is it held in its place of priority? I believe the greater the pressure, the greater your need for time alone with Him.
Kay Arthur

Your Source of Strength

Cast your burden upon the Lord and He will sustain you;
He will never allow the righteous to be shaken.
Psalm 55:22 NASB

When you find yourself worried about the challenges of today or the uncertainties of tomorrow, ask yourself whether you're ready to place your concerns and your life in God's all-powerful, all-knowing, all-loving hands. If the answer to that question is yes, then you can draw strength today from the source of strength that never fails—your Father in heaven.

Even when trouble arrives at your door and threatens an extended stay, you can find comfort and courage in the certain knowledge that your Creator is keenly aware of your pain—and that He is willing and able to heal your broken heart.

So when tough times come, depend on God. He is trustworthy, now and forever.

Seeing that a Pilot steers the ship in which we sail, who will never allow us to perish even in the midst of shipwrecks, there is no reason why our minds should be overwhelmed with fear and overcome with weariness.

John Calvin

Solving the Riddles

If any of you lacks wisdom, you should ask God, who gives generously to all without finding fault, and it will be given to you.

James 1:5 TNIV

Are you facing a difficult decision? Life presents each of us with countless questions, conundrums, doubts, and problems. Thankfully, the riddles of everyday living are not too difficult to solve if we look for answers in the right places. When we have questions, we can consult God's Word, seek the guidance of the Holy Spirit, and ask advice from God-fearing friends and family members.

Take your concerns to God, and avail yourself of the messages and mentors He has placed along your path. When you do, God will speak to you in His own way and in His own time. And when He does, you can trust the answers He gives.

Never make a decision without stopping to consider the matter in the presence of God.

Josemaria Escriva

Passing Through the Storms of Life

Jesus responded, "Why are you afraid?
You have so little faith!"
Then he got up and rebuked the wind and waves,
and suddenly there was a great calm.
Matthew 8:26 NLT

Sometimes, like Jesus's disciples, we feel threatened by the storms of life. During these moments, when our hearts are flooded with uncertainty, we must remember that God is not far off: He's right here with us.

Have you ever felt your faith in God slipping away? Even the most faithful Christians are, at times, beset by occasional bouts of discouragement and doubt. But even when you feel far removed from God, He never leaves your side. He is always with you, always strong enough to calm your life's storms—and even use them for your good. When you sincerely seek His presence—and when you genuinely endeavor to establish a deeper, more meaningful relationship with God—He will calm your fears, answer your prayers, and restore your soul.

God will make obstacles serve His purpose.
Lettie B. Cowman

The Courage to Dream

It is pleasant to see dreams come true,
but fools refuse to turn from evil to attain them.
Proverbs 13:19 NLT

It takes courage to dream big dreams. You will discover that courage when you do three things: accept the past, trust God to handle the future, and make the most of the time He has given you today.

How big are you willing to dream? Do you believe that God can perform miracles in your own life and in the lives of your loved ones? Are you willing to ask Him to move mountains in your life? Are you willing to do the work He requires? Hopefully so. After all, no dreams are too big for God—not even yours.

So don't lose another day, another hour, or another minute. Start dreaming big dreams today. Then start working—and praying—to make those dreams come true.

If one advances confidently in the direction of his dreams, and endeavors to live the life he has imagined, he will meet with success
unexpected in common hours.
Henry David Thoreau

Sharing Words of Hope

Let's see how inventive we can be in encouraging love and helping out, not avoiding worshiping together as some do but spurring each other on.
Hebrews 10:24–25 MSG

Are you a hopeful, optimistic, encouraging person? And do you associate with like-minded people?

Hope, like other human emotions, is contagious. When we associate with hope-filled friends, we are encouraged by their faith and optimism. But if we spend too much time in the company of naysayers and pessimists, our attitudes, like theirs, will tend toward the cynical and negative.

As a child of God, you have every reason to be hopeful—and you have every reason to share your hope with others. So today, look for reasons to celebrate. And while you're at it, look for people who will join you in the celebration of God's blessings. As you share hope, you'll build hope.

We urgently need people who encourage and inspire us to move toward God.
Jim Cymbala

Serenity Now

The Lord says, . . . "Do not think about the past. Look at the new thing I am going to do. It is already happening. Don't you see it? I will make a road in the desert and rivers in the dry land."

Isaiah 43:18–19 NCV

Theologian Reinhold Niebuhr composed a profoundly simple verse known as the Serenity Prayer: "God grant me the serenity to accept the things I cannot change, the courage to change the things I can, and the wisdom to know the difference." Niebuhr's words are far easier to recite than to live by. Why? Because most of us want life to unfold in accordance with our own wishes and timetables. But sometimes God has other plans.

When events transpire that are beyond our control, we have a choice: we can either learn to accept and trust, or we can make ourselves miserable as we struggle to change the unchangeable.

Today, ask God to give you the wisdom and courage to accept life as it comes. Trust Him to provide what you need, and you'll find real serenity.

Have courage for the great sorrows of life and patience for the small ones; and when you have laboriously accomplished your daily task, go to sleep in peace. God is awake.

Victor Hugo

Faith to Share

This and this only has been my appointed work:
getting this news to those who have never heard
of God, and explaining how it works
by simple faith and plain truth.

1 Timothy 2:7 MSG

Genuine faith was never meant to be locked up inside our hearts—to the contrary, it is meant to be shared with the world. Of course, if you wish to share your faith, you first must find it.

How can you find and strengthen your faith? Through praise, through worship, through fellowship, through Bible study, and through prayer. When you do these things, your faith will become stronger, and you'll find ways to share that faith with family members, with friends, and with the world.

So today, spend precious moments with your heavenly Father. And then share your faith and your enthusiasm with a world that needs both.

Our faith becomes stronger as we express it;
a growing faith is a sharing faith.

Billy Graham

While It Is Day

While it is daytime, we must continue doing
the work of the One who sent me.
Night is coming, when no one can work.
John 9:4 NCV

The words of John 9:4 remind us that "night is coming" for all of us. But when we take God at His Word—and when we take comfort in His promises—we need never fear the night. After all, the Father has promised to love us and protect us. Armed with these assurances, we can face life courageously, seizing the opportunities He places before us each day.

Today is a priceless gift that has been given to you by God—don't waste it. Don't stand on the sidelines as life's parade passes you by. Instead, search for the possibilities God has placed along your path. This day is a one-of-a-kind treasure that can be put to good use—or wasted. Your challenge is to use this day joyfully and productively. And while you're at it, encourage others to do likewise. After all, night is coming.

The whole essence of the spiritual life consists in
recognizing the designs of God for us
at the present moment.
Elisabeth Elliot

Infinite Forgiveness

Forgive us our sins, for we also forgive everyone who is indebted to us.

Luke 11:4 NKJV

God's power to forgive is infinite—as is His love. Despite our shortcomings, despite our mistakes, God offers us immediate forgiveness when we ask Him. Despite our past failures, despite our weaknesses, God loves us still.

Because God has forgiven us—because He loves us in spite of our imperfections and frailties—we too should be quick to forgive others. As recipients of God's mercy, we should be merciful. When we offer forgiveness to others, God grants us the peace and contentment He wants us to know.

So when it comes to forgiveness, remember two simple truths: God offers His forgiveness to us; and we should offer our forgiveness to others.

It's as simple—and as wonderful—as that.

Our forgiveness toward others should flow from a realization and appreciation of God's forgiveness toward us.

Franklin Graham

In His Hands

Don't brashly announce what you're going to do tomorrow;
you don't know the first thing about tomorrow.
Proverbs 27:1 MSG

The world turns according to God's plans, not our wishes. No matter how carefully we plan, our plans may go amiss. So boasting about future events is best avoided, especially when we understand and acknowledge God's sovereignty over all things.

Are you planning for a better tomorrow for yourself and your family? That's natural and even commendable; God rewards forethought just as He rebukes impulsiveness. The key is to submit all of our desires and plans to God's perfect will for our lives, knowing that He knows best.

So as you make your plans, do so with humility, consulting with and trusting in your heavenly Father. It's His hand that directs the future.

That we may not complain of what is,
let us see God's hand in all events; and,
that we may not be afraid of what shall be,
let us see all events in God's hand.
Matthew Henry

His Rule, Your Rule

Here is a simple, rule-of-thumb guide for behavior:
Ask yourself what you want people to do for you,
then grab the initiative and do it for them.
Add up God's Law and Prophets and this is what you get.
Matthew 7:12 MSG

How do you treat your friends and family members? Is the Golden Rule your rule?

Jesus instructed us to treat other people in the same way we want to be treated. Yet sometimes, when we're feeling the pressures of everyday living, living by the Golden Rule can seem like an impossible task—but it's not.

Would you like to improve the quality of your life? Would you like to make the world a better place at the same time? If so, you can start by practicing God's Golden Rule. When you want to know how to treat other people, ask the person you see every time you look in the mirror. The answer you receive will tell you exactly what to do.

It is wrong for anyone to be anxious to receive
more from his neighbor than he himself
is willing to give to God.
Saint Francis of Assisi

Your Way or God's Way

A man's heart plans his way,
but the Lord directs his steps.
Proverbs 16:9 NKJV

The popular song "My Way" is a perfectly good tune, but it's a less-than-perfect guide for life. If you're looking for life's perfect prescription, forget about doing things your way and start doing things God's way.

As you consider the path He wants you to follow, you will periodically ask yourself, "What now, Lord?" If you earnestly seek God's will for your life, you will find it . . . in time.

Sometimes God's plans are crystal clear; sometimes they're not. So be patient, keep searching, and keep praying. If you do, God will answer your prayers and make His plans known. The more you do things His way, the more He'll reveal His way. Step by step, God will direct you . . . and there's no better way.

He knows when we go into the storm,
He watches over us in the storm, and He can
bring us out of the storm when His purposes
have been fulfilled.
Warren Wiersbe

Ultimate Wisdom

Happy is the person who finds wisdom,
the one who gets understanding.
Proverbs 3:13 NCV

When you find wisdom—and when you apply that wisdom to the challenges of everyday living—you'll enrich your own life and the lives of your loved ones. But the acquisition of wisdom is seldom easy or quick.

Wisdom is not like a mushroom; it doesn't spring up overnight. It's more like an oak tree that starts as a tiny acorn, grows into a sapling, and then, after many years, reaches up to the sky, tall and strong.

Do you seek wisdom? Then seek it every day of your life. Seek it with consistency and perseverance. And, most importantly, seek it in the right place. That place is, first and foremost, the Word of God.

If you study God's teachings, you will find the understanding you seek. And you'll find that no other source is adequate: God's wisdom is the ultimate wisdom.

Love Holy Scripture, and wisdom will love you.
Love Scripture, and she will keep you.
Honor her, and she will keep you.
Saint Augustine

March 23

The Right Kind of Habits

Who among you is wise and understanding?
Let him show by his good behavior his deeds
in the gentleness of wisdom.
James 3:13 NASB

It's an old saying and a true one: first you make your habits, and then your habits make you. Some habits will bring you closer to God; other habits will lead you away from Him and the path He has chosen for you. If you sincerely desire to improve your spiritual health, you must honestly examine the habits that make up the fabric of your day. And you must abandon any habits that are displeasing to God.

If you trust your heavenly Father, and if you ask for His help, He can transform your life. If you sincerely seek Him, the same God who created the universe will help you defeat the harmful habits that have heretofore defeated you. So if at first you don't succeed, keep praying. God is listening, and He's ready to help you become a better person—the kind of person He created you to be.

Habits are like a cable. We weave a strand every day and soon it cannot be broken.
Horace Mann

Never Lose Hope

These things I have spoken to you, that in Me you may have peace. In the world you will have tribulation; but be of good cheer, I have overcome the world.

John 16:33 NKJV

There are few sadder sights on earth than the sight of a person who has lost all hope. But if you place your faith in God, you need never lose hope. After all, God is good; His love endures; He has promised us the gift of eternal life; and He always keeps His promises.

If you find yourself falling into the spiritual traps of worry and discouragement, consider the words of Jesus. He said, "I have overcome the world." Our world is indeed a place of trials and tribulations, but if we put our trust in God, we will be secure. God has promised us peace and joy. It's up to us to claim these gifts.

It's time for you to claim these gifts today . . . and never lose hope.

When you say a situation or a person is hopeless, you are slamming the door in the face of God.

Charles Allen

The Temptation to Judge

When they continued to ask Jesus their question,
he raised up and said, "Anyone here who has
never sinned can throw the first stone at her."
John 8:7 NCV

As Jesus came upon a young woman who had been condemned by the religious leaders, He told the people gathered there that only the person who was without sin should cast the first stone. His message applied not only to those Pharisees of ancient times but also to us. If we genuinely want to experience God's peace and His joy, we must leave the judging to Him.

If you'd like to live a more peaceful, joyful existence, here's one important step you should take: resist the temptation to judge others. Don't gossip, don't denigrate, don't belittle, and don't malign. Instead, spend your time sharing God's love and spreading His message. After all, none of us is perfect. The world could use fewer judges and more witnesses . . . folks like you . . . who are willing to share God's good news.

Forget the faults of others
by remembering your own.
John Bunyan

Respecting Yourself

To acquire wisdom is to love oneself;
people who cherish understanding will prosper.
Proverbs 19:8 NLT

Do you place a high value on your time and your talents? You should. After all, you were created by God with an array of unique gifts and opportunities, all of which He wants you to use effectively and efficiently. But if you've acquired the unfortunate habit of devaluing your efforts or yourself, it's time to revolutionize the way you think about your career, your capabilities, your opportunities, and your future.

Nobody can build up your self-confidence if you're unwilling to believe in your value as a child of God. And the world won't give you much respect until you show appropriate respect for yourself. So if you've been talking yourself down or selling yourself short, stop. Remember this: The God of the whole universe handcrafted you! You are precious in His sight.

The first and worst of all frauds is to cheat one's self.
All sin is easy after that.
Pearl Bailey

Calming Your Fears

Do not be afraid; only believe.
Mark 5:36 NKJV

Most of the things we worry about will never come to pass—yet we worry still. We worry about the future and the past; we worry about finances and relationships. As we survey the landscape of our lives, we observe all manner of molehills and imagine them to be mountains.

Are you concerned about the challenges looming ahead? If so, why not ask God to help you regain a clear perspective about the problems (and opportunities) that confront you? When you petition your heavenly Father sincerely and seek His guidance, He can touch your heart, clear your vision, renew your mind, and calm your fears.

Courage faces fear and thereby masters it.
Cowardice represses fear and is thereby
mastered by it.
Martin Luther King Jr.

In Focus

Look straight ahead, and fix your eyes on what lies before you. Mark out a straight path for your feet; stay on the safe path. Don't get sidetracked; keep your feet from following evil.

Proverbs 4:25–27 NLT

This day—and every day—is a chance to celebrate the life God has given you. It's also a chance to give thanks to the One who has offered you more blessings than you can possibly count. So what is your focus today? Are you willing to turn your thoughts to God's blessings and embrace His promises? Or will you focus your energies on other things?

Today, why not fix your eyes on the comfort and joy that can be yours? Why not take time to celebrate God's glorious creation? Why not entrust all your hopes and fears to your heavenly Father? When you do, you'll be able to think more optimistically and faithfully about yourself and your world . . . and then you can share your faith-based optimism with others. They'll be better for it, and so will you.

The greatest honor we can give Almighty God is to live gladly because of the knowledge of His love.

Juliana of Norwich

Getting to Know Him

Take up My yoke and learn from Me, because I am gentle and humble in heart, and you will find rest for yourselves. For My yoke is easy and My burden is light.

Matthew 11:29–30 HCSB

Oswald Chambers, author of the Christian classic devotional text My *Utmost for His Highest*, advised: "Never support an experience which does not have God as its source, and faith in God as its result." These words serve as a powerful reminder that we are called to walk with God and to obey His commandments. God gave us those commandments for a reason: not to oppress us, but so that we might obey them and be blessed.

We live in a world that presents us with countless temptations to stray far from God's path. But if we're wise, we will defend ourselves against and resist these temptations. God has given us clear instructions for when we're confronted with sin: we should walk–or, better yet, run–in the opposite direction. The good news is, the better we know Him, the easier–and more comforting–that will be.

Bible history is filled with people who began the race with great success but failed at the end because they disregarded God's rules.

Warren Wiersbe

April

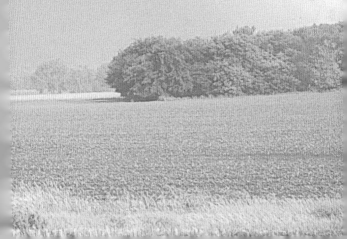

God's Wisdom and Your Finances

It is better to get wisdom than gold,
and to choose understanding rather than silver!
Proverbs 16:16 NCV

If you've ever experienced money troubles, you know all about the sleepless nights that can accompany financial hardship. But the good news is this: your heavenly Father is ready, willing, and perfectly able to help you overcome every kind of problem, including the monetary kind.

Ours is a society in love with money and the things money can buy. But God cares about people, not possessions . . . and He cares about you. So study what God's Word has to say about discipline and about money. Pray about your resources. Ask the Creator for wisdom to spend wisely and strength to work diligently. Then do whatever it takes to live in accordance with *all* of God's teachings. When you do, you'll experience the peace—both financial and spiritual—that only God can provide.

If a person gets his attitude toward money straight,
it will help straighten out almost
every other area in his life.
Billy Graham

An Offer of Peace

Peace I leave with you; My peace I give to you;
not as the world gives do I give to you.
Do not let your heart be troubled, nor let it be fearful.
John 14:27 NASB

The beautiful words of John 14:27 remind us that God offers us peace–not the kind the world offers, but rather the kind as He alone can give. This peace is a precious gift from our Creator. All we have to do is to trust Him and accept that gift with praise on our lips and gratitude in our hearts.

Have you found the genuine peace that can be yours through a relationship with God? Or are you still rushing after the illusion of peace and happiness that the world promises but cannot deliver?

Today, as a gift to yourself, to your family, and to your friends, open your heart to God's peace. It is offered freely; it has been paid for in full; it is yours for the asking.

Where the soul is full of peace and joy, outward surroundings and circumstances are of comparatively little account.
Hannah Whitall Smith

Lost in the Crowd

The fear of human opinion disables;
trusting in God protects you from that.
Proverbs 29:25 MSG

Whom will you try to please today: your God or your associates? Best-selling author and pastor Rick Warren observed, "Those who follow the crowd usually get lost in it." We know these words to be true, yet often we fail to live by them. Instead of trusting God for guidance, we imitate our neighbors. And if we're not careful, we can place popularity above principles. Instead of seeking to please our Father in heaven, we strive to please our peers.

Our obligation is not to please or impress neighbors, friends, or even family members. Our obligation is to please an all-knowing, all-powerful God. When we do that and trust Him, we won't be crippled by fear of what others think.

Today and always, seek first to please your loving, heavenly Father. Then you'll never get lost in the crowd.

There is nothing that makes more cowards and
feeble men than public opinion.
Henry Ward Beecher

A Time to Rest

*Come to Me, all you who labor and are heavy laden,
and I will give you rest. Take My yoke upon you
and learn from Me, for I am gentle and lowly in heart,
and you will find rest for your souls.
For My yoke is easy and My burden is light.*
Matthew 11:28–30 NKJV

Physical exhaustion is God's way of telling us to slow down. Yes, God expects us to work hard, but He also intends for us to rest. When we fail to take the rest we need, we do a disservice to ourselves and to our families, and we don't live according to God's plan.

We live in a world that tempts us to stay up late—very late. But too much late-night TV, combined with too little sleep, is a prescription for exhaustion.

Are your physical or spiritual batteries running low? Is your energy on the wane? Are your emotions frayed? If so, it's time to turn your thoughts and prayers to God. And when you're finished, it's probably time to turn off the lights and go to bed!

Prescription for a happier and healthier life: resolve to slow down your pace; learn to say no gracefully; resist the temptation to chase after more pleasure, more hobbies, and more social entanglements.
James Dobson

The Shepherd's Gift

My cup runs over. Surely goodness and mercy shall follow me all the days of my life; and I will dwell in the house of the Lord forever.
Psalm 23:5–6 NKJV

When we entrust our hearts and our days to God, we'll experience His abundance and His comfort. But when we turn our thoughts and direct our energies away from God, we forfeit the comfort that might otherwise be ours.

Do you sincerely seek the spiritual riches the Creator offers to those who give themselves to Him? Do you want to enjoy the confidence and assurance that result from a genuine, life-altering relationship with a loving Father? Then trust Him completely, and follow Him without reservation. When you do, you will receive the love and abundance He has promised.

Today, and every day hereafter, open your heart to God. Let Him fill it with the joy, the comfort, and the blessings the Shepherd offers His sheep.

God cannot give us a happiness and peace apart from Himself, because it is not there. There is no such thing.
C. S. Lewis

Face-to-Face with Old Man Trouble

When you go through deep waters, I will be with you. When you go through rivers of difficulty, you will not drown. When you walk through the fire of oppression, you will not be burned up; the flames will not consume you. For I am the Lord, your God.

Isaiah 43:2–3 NLT

All of us encounter occasional setbacks—those inevitable visits from Old Man Trouble from which none of us are exempt. The fact that we encounter adversity is not nearly as important as the way we choose to deal with it.

When tough times arrive, we have to make a choice: we can choose to begin the difficult work of tackling our troubles . . . or we can choose to cower in the corner. When we summon the courage to look Old Man Trouble squarely in the eye, more often than not, he blinks . . . and sometimes he even retreats. God, on the other hand, never leaves us—not even for a moment. God's love never falters, and it never fails and because God remains steadfast, we have great comfort even in the midst of trouble and we can live courageously.

The closer we are to God, the more confidence we place in him when we are under fire.

C. H. Spurgeon

The Real You

We justify our actions by appearances;
God examines our motives.
Proverbs 21:2 MSG

The world sees you as you appear to be; God sees you as you really are. He knows your heart, and He understands your intentions. The opinions of others should be relatively unimportant to you, but God's view of you–of your actions, your thoughts, and your motivations–should be vitally important.

Few things in life are more futile than "keeping up appearances" for the sake of others. What is important is pleasing our Father in heaven while we provide support and encouragement to our family members and our closest friends.

Today, do yourself a favor: Worry less about physical appearances and more about spiritual realities. Take comfort in knowing your Father sees–and loves–the real you.

The life of a good religious person ought to abound in
every virtue so that he is, on the interior,
what to others he appears to be.
Thomas à Kempis

April 8

Belief and Behavior

If we live in the Spirit, let us also walk in the Spirit.

Galatians 5:25 NKJV

It's never enough for us to simply hear God's instructions; we must also live by them. Do you believe the words of God? Does your behavior match your beliefs?

Today, don't treat your faith as if it were separate from your everyday life. Weave your beliefs into the very fabric of your day. Make every encounter an opportunity to serve; make every word an effort to encourage family, friends, and even strangers. When you do, God will honor your good works, and your good works will honor God.

Don't be afraid to stand up for your beliefs. Remember this: in the battle of vice versus virtue, the opposition never takes a day off . . . but neither does God. He'll comfort and strengthen you to live out His instructions for a faithful life.

We must, without apology, without fear, without ceasing, preach and practice our beliefs, carrying them out to the point of suffering.

R. G. Lee

Taking Care of Your Temple

Don't you know that you are God's temple
and that God's Spirit lives in you?
1 Corinthians 3:16 NCV

God has a plan for every aspect of our lives, and His plan includes provisions for our physical well-being. But He expects us to do our fair share of the work! We live in a world in which leisure is glorified and consumption is commercialized. But God has better plans for His children. He does not intend for us to take our health for granted. To the contrary, He wants us to treat our bodies like temples . . . because that's precisely what they are. Our bodies are God's temple.

In a world that is chock-full of tasty temptations, it's all too easy to make unhealthy choices. Our challenge is to resist those unhealthy temptations. Self-discipline is one means of doing that, but so is prayer. Today, ask your Creator to help you take care of the body He so carefully and wonderfully created. When you ask for God's help, He will give it—and you'll feel better inside and out.

God wants you to give Him your body.
Some people do foolish things with their bodies. God
wants your body as a holy sacrifice.
Warren Wiersbe

Character Counts

Lead a quiet and peaceable life in all godliness and honesty.
1 Timothy 2:2 KJV

When we seek to live each day with discipline, honesty, and faith, at least two things happen: integrity becomes a habit, and God blesses us because of our obedience to Him.

Living a life of integrity isn't always the easiest way, but it is always the right way . . . and God clearly intends that it should be our way.

Character is the sum of every right decision, every honest word, every noble thought, and every heartfelt prayer. It is forged on the anvil of honorable work and polished by the twin virtues of generosity and humility. Character is built slowly over a lifetime and is a precious thing–difficult to develop, wonderful to witness. As thoughtful adults, we must seek to live each day with discipline, honesty, and faith. When we do, integrity becomes a habit. And God smiles.

Character cannot be developed in ease and quiet. Only through trial and suffering is the soul strengthened.
Helen Keller

Choosing Wisely

The wisdom that is from above is first pure, then peaceable, gentle, willing to yield, full of mercy and good fruits, without partiality and without hypocrisy.

James 3:17 NKJV

Because we possess free will, we make choices—lots of them. When we make choices that are pleasing to our heavenly Father, we are blessed. When we make choices that keep us following in the footsteps of God's Son, we enjoy the abundance Jesus promised to those who follow Him. But when we make choices that are displeasing to God, we sow seeds that have the potential to bring forth an unhappy harvest.

Today, as you encounter the challenges of everyday living, you will make hundreds of choices. Choose wisely. Remember that every choice that is displeasing to God is the wrong choice—no exceptions. So make your thoughts and your actions pleasing to God. Then you'll know the deep comforts of His pleasure and peace.

We are either the masters or the victims of our attitudes. It is a matter of personal choice. Who we are today is the result of choices we made yesterday. Tomorrow, we will become what we choose today.

John Maxwell

The Greatest of These

These three remain: faith, hope and love.
But the greatest of these is love.
1 Corinthians 13:13 NIV

The familiar words of 1 Corinthians 13 remind us of the importance of love. Faith is vital, of course. So too is hope. But love is more important still.

Jesus showed His love for us on the cross, and we are called upon to return His love by sharing it. We are to love one another just as Christ loved us (John 13:34). That's a tall order, but we must follow it.

Sometimes love is easy (puppies and sleeping children come to mind), and sometimes love is hard (fallible human beings come to mind). But God's Word is clear: we are to love all our friends and neighbors, not just the "lovable" ones. So today, take time to spread God's message–and His love–by word and by example. It's not easy, but it's the greatest thing you can do.

The cross symbolizes a cosmic as well as
a historic truth. Love conquers the world,
but its victory is not an easy one.
Reinhold Neibuhr

Need Directions?

Man does not live on bread alone,
but on every word that comes from the mouth of God.
Matthew 4:4 NIV

As you look to the future and decide upon the direction of your life, what will you use as your road map? Will you trust God's Word and use it as an indispensable tool to guide your steps? Or will you choose a different map to plot your course? The map you choose will determine the quality of your journey and its ultimate destination.

The Bible is the ultimate guidebook for life—and that's precisely how you should use it. So today and every day, consult God's instruction book with an open mind and a prayerful heart. When you do, you can take comfort in the knowledge that your steps are guided by a source of wisdom that never fails.

I believe the Bible is the best gift
God has ever given to men.
Abraham Lincoln

Genuine Comfort

The Lord gives strength to his people;
the Lord blesses his people with peace.
Psalm 29:11 NIV

Everywhere we turn, or so it seems, the world promises us contentment and happiness. But the contentment the world offers is fleeting and incomplete. Thankfully, the contentment God offers is all-encompassing and everlasting.

Happiness depends less upon our circumstances than upon our thoughts. When we turn our thoughts to God, to His gifts, and to His glorious creation, we experience the comfort and joy God intends for us to experience. But when we focus on the negative aspects of life–or when we disobey God's instructions–we cause ourselves needless suffering.

Do you sincerely want to be a contented person? Then set your mind and your heart upon God's love and His grace . . . and let Him take care of the rest.

When you accept rather than fight your circumstances, even though you don't understand them, you open your heart's gate to God's love, peace, joy, and contentment.
Amy Carmichael

During Difficult Days

It will be hard when all these things happen to you. But after that you will come back to the Lord your God and obey him, because the Lord your God is a merciful God. He will not leave you or destroy you. He will not forget the Agreement with your ancestors, which he swore to them.

Deuteronomy 4:30–31 NCV

Sometimes the traffic jams, and sometimes the dog gobbles the homework. But when we find ourselves mired in the minor frustrations of life, we must catch ourselves, take a deep breath, and lift our thoughts upward. Although we are here on earth struggling to rise above the distractions of the day, we need never struggle alone. God is here–eternally and faithfully, with infinite patience and love–and if we reach out to Him, He will restore perspective and peace to our souls.

If you find yourself in difficult circumstances, remember that God is merciful and faithful. If you become discouraged with the direction of your day, or your life, lift your thoughts and prayers to Him. He will comfort you and guide you through your difficulties . . . and beyond them.

When life is difficult, God wants us to have a faith that trusts and waits.

Kay Arthur

Expressing Your Emotions

There is a time for everything . . . a time to weep and a time to laugh, a time to mourn and a time to dance.

Ecclesiastes 3:1, 4 NIV

God gave us emotions, and He intends for us to express them. When we express our emotions sincerely, we can bring joy or even begin the process of healing. But if we suppress our emotions, or if we ignore our feelings altogether, we may needlessly prolong our pain.

If you've experienced a significant loss or a profound disappointment, don't bottle up everything inside. Express your feelings; talk openly to loved ones; allow tears to flow. Even if you'd rather ignore your pain, don't do it. Reach out to the people you love and trust.

By honestly expressing your grief, you will take an active role in God's plan for your recovery. And in time, you'll experience the comfort and the joy that can be yours—and that God wants you to know.

Christians are told not to stifle their grief or to behave unscripturally stoic.

Charles Stanley

No Pity Parties

The nights of crying your eyes out give way to days of laughter.

Psalm 30:5 MSG

Self-pity is not only an unproductive way to think; it's also an affront to our Father in heaven. God's Word promises that His children can receive peace, comfort, love, and eternal life. These gifts are an outpouring from God, a manifestation of His grace. With these rich blessings, how can we possibly feel sorry for ourselves?

Self-pity and peace cannot coexist in the same mind. Bitterness and joy cannot coexist in the same heart. Thanksgiving and despair are mutually exclusive. So if you're allowing thoughts of pain and worry to dominate your life, train yourself to think less about your troubles and more about God's blessings. Hasn't He given you enough blessings to occupy your thoughts all day, every day, from now on? Of course He has! So focus your mind on Him, and skip the pity party. You have better things to do!

A complete holiday from self-pity is necessary to success.

Dorothea Brande

Friendships That Honor God

Blessed is the man who walks not in the counsel of the ungodly, nor stands in the path of sinners, nor sits in the seat of the scornful; but his delight is in the law of the Lord, and in His law he meditates day and night.

Psalm 1:1–2 NKJV

Because we tend to become like our friends, we must choose those friends carefully. Some friends encourage us to work hard, to behave rationally, to do the right thing, and to honor God. These friendships should be nurtured. Other friends may place us in situations where we're likely to get into trouble—that kind of friendship has the potential to do us harm, perhaps great harm.

Since our friends influence us in ways that are both subtle and powerful, we must ensure that our friendships are pleasing to God. When we spend our days in the presence of spiritually minded and clearheaded comrades, we'll be comforted and blessed—not only by those friends, but also by our Creator.

I have found that the closer I am to the godly people around me, the easier it is for me to live a righteous life because they hold me accountable.

John MacArthur

Family Honor

Show family affection to one another with brotherly love. Outdo one another in showing honor.

Romans 12:10 HCSB

She was born Erma Louise Fiste, but if you're old enough to remember the 1970s, '80s, and '90s, you probably remember her by her married name Erma Bombeck—once one of America's most popular commentators and humorists.

Erma once described her family this way: "Our strange little band of characters trudging through life sharing diseases, toothpaste, coveting one another's desserts, hiding shampoo, locking each other out of rooms, loving, laughing, defending, and trying to figure out the common thread that bound us all together."

That certainly sounds like a typical family. If you're lucky enough to be a part of such a clan, give thanks to your heavenly Father and show affection and honor to your earthly family. After all, who knows when you might need some toothpaste . . . or a hug?

What can we do to promote world peace? Go home and love your family.

Mother Teresa

April 20

Expecting the Best

We are saved by hope.

Romans 8:24 KJV

Do you believe that God has wonderful things in store for you and your loved ones? You should, because He does. So as you plan for the next stage of your life's journey, promise yourself that when it comes to the truly important things in life, you won't settle for second best. What are the "important things"? Your faith, your family, and your relationships, for starters. In each of these areas, determine to be a rip-roaring, top-drawer success.

If you've entrusted your life to God, you have every reason to be hopeful. And if you remain faithful to His teachings and open to His love, you can expect to receive His richest blessings. So set God-centered goals (prayerfully), work hard (faithfully), and dare to dream (confidently). When you do, you can expect, through faith, to receive God's best gifts. Not second best . . . *the best.*

Hope is nothing more than the expectation of those things which faith has believed to be truly promised by God.

John Calvin

Saying Yes to God

Fear not, for I am with you.
Isaiah 41:10 NKJV

Your decision to seek a deeper relationship with God won't remove all problems from your life; to the contrary, it may bring about a series of personal crises as you constantly seek to say yes to God when the world pressures you to do otherwise. Each time you are tempted to distance yourself from the Creator, you face a spiritual crisis. A few of these crises may be monumental in scope, but most will be the small, everyday decisions of life. In fact, life can be seen as one test after another–and with each crisis comes yet another opportunity to grow closer to God . . . or to distance yourself from His plan for your life.

Today you will face many opportunities to say yes to God–and you will encounter many opportunities to say no to Him. Your answers will determine not only the quality of your day but also the direction of your life. Step out in faith, and just say yes!

God provides for those who trust.
George Herbert

Making Difficulties Disappear

We also rejoice in our afflictions, because we know that affliction produces endurance, endurance produces proven character, and proven character produces hope.

Romans 5:3–4 HCSB

John Quincy Adams observed, "Courage and perseverance have a magical talisman, before which difficulties disappear and obstacles vanish into air." When we attack our problems courageously—and keep attacking them—the result of our endurance will often bring success. But we know it's a matter of perseverance, not prestidigitation.

Do you seek a "magic talisman" that will help ensure that you receive the rewards you desire from life? No need to look in the local magic shop; instead, look to God and ask Him to give you strength to keep working even when you'd rather quit. Find the courage to stand firm in the face of adversity. In the end, only faith, courage, and perseverance are proven effective at making problems disappear.

Press on. Obstacles are seldom the same size tomorrow as they are today.

Robert Schuller

His Rightful Place

You shall have no other gods before Me.
Exodus 20:3 NKJV

As you think about the nature of your relationship with God, remember this: you will always have some type of relationship with Him. It's unavoidable; your life will be lived in relation to God. The question is not whether you will have a relationship with Him; the question is whether that relationship will be one that seeks to honor Him.

Are you willing to place God first in your life? Are you willing to welcome Him into your heart? Unless you can honestly answer these questions with a resounding yes, your relationship with God isn't what it could be or should be. But God is always available, and He's always ready to forgive. He offers greater comfort and blessing than you'll find anywhere else. Your heavenly Father loves you and wants a close relationship with you, not a distant one. He's waiting to hear from you now. Will you call on Him?

When you use your life for God's glory,
everything you do can become an act of worship.
Rick Warren

April 24

Take Time to Be Kind

As those who have been chosen of God, holy and beloved, put on a heart of compassion, kindness, humility, gentleness and patience.

Colossians 3:12 NASB

The instructions of Colossians 3:12 are unambiguous: we are to be compassionate, humble, gentle, and kind. But sometimes, when the pressures of daily life weigh heavily upon our shoulders, we fall short. Amid the busyness and confusion of our everyday responsibilities, we may neglect to share a kind word or a kind deed. This oversight hurts others, yes, but perhaps it hurts us most of all.

Today, slow down enough to be alert to those who need comforting words, a helping hand, or a heartfelt hug. Make kindness a hallmark of your dealings with others. They will be blessed, you will be blessed, and God will be honored.

Kind words can be short and easy to speak, but their echoes are truly endless.

Mother Teresa

Working to Become the Best You

First plant your fields; then build your barn.
Proverbs 24:27 MSG

Helen Hayes said, "My mother drew a distinction between achievement and success. She said that achievement is the knowledge that you have studied and worked hard and done the best that is in you. Success is being praised by others. Success is nice but not as important or satisfying. Always aim for achievement and forget about success."

Miss Hayes's mother was wise indeed.

Success in God's eyes lies in the ability to place more importance on doing the work He has set before you than on striving for recognition. So if you want to be a true success, forget about being successful. Concentrate, instead, on honoring God by doing your best and becoming the best "you" you can be. Your Creator has bestowed you with gifts–and he wants you to use them.

The great law of culture: Let each become all that he was created capable of being.
Thomas Carlyle

New Beginnings

I will give you a new heart and put a new spirit in you.
Ezekiel 36:26 NIV

If we sincerely want to change for the better, we must start on the inside and work our way out from there. Lasting change doesn't occur "out there"; it occurs "in here." It takes place not in the shifting sands of our situation but in the quiet depths of our hearts.

Life is constantly changing. Our circumstances change; our opportunities change; our responsibilities change; and our relationships change. Sometimes, when we reach the crossroads of life, we may feel the need for a jump start—or the need to start over from scratch.

Are you in search of a new beginning, or even a new you? If so, don't be fooled into thinking that new circumstances will miraculously transform you into the person you want to become. Transformation comes only from God, and it begins in the humble human heart. If you feel the need for a fresh start, talk to God today. He specializes in new beginnings.

God is not running an antique shop!
He is making all things new!
Vance Havner

Keeping Up with the Joneses

A pretentious, showy life is an empty life;
a plain and simple life is a full life.
Proverbs 13:7 MSG

As a member of this highly competitive, twenty-first-century world, you know that the demands and expectations of everyday living can seem overwhelming at times. Keeping up with the Joneses can become a full-time job. A better strategy is to stop trying to please the neighbors and to concentrate on pleasing God.

Perhaps you've set your goals high; if so, congratulations! You're willing to dream big dreams, and that's a good thing. But as you consider your life's purpose, don't allow your quest for excellence to interfere with the spiritual journey God has planned for you. Strive to please God first and always. How? By welcoming Him into your heart and by following His lead. All other concerns will fall into proper perspective when we keep our eyes on God.

Amition! We must be careful what we mean by it. If it means the desire to get ahead of other people—which is what I think it does mean—then it is bad. If it simply means wanting to do a thing well, then it is good.

C. S. Lewis

Make Prayer a Habit

Let everyone who is godly pray to You.
Psalm 32:6 NASB

Is prayer an integral part of your daily life, or is it a hit-or-miss habit? Do you "pray without ceasing," or is your prayer life an afterthought? Do you regularly pray in the solitude of the early morning darkness, or do you lower your head only at mealtimes, when others are watching? The quantity and the quality of your prayer life will affect the rest of your life, for good or ill.

Prayer is a powerful tool for spiritual growth and a powerful tool for changing your world. So here's a challenge: make prayer a habit. Begin early in the morning, even if you don't have a lot of time, and continue throughout the day. Remember, God does answer prayer; but He's not likely to grant requests you haven't made. Spend time with your heavenly Father today.

There are times when we simply don't feel like praying—
and that is when we need to pray the most!
Warren Wiersbe

Mature Righteousness

Run away from infantile indulgence. Run after mature righteousness—faith, love, peace—joining those who are in honest and serious prayer before God.

2 Timothy 2:22 MSG

An important part of growing up is learning the wisdom of doing what needs to be done when it needs to be done. The better part of maturity is understanding the value of doing the right thing . . . and that means living in accordance with God's instructions.

God's Word teaches us to be faithful, honest, generous, disciplined, loving, kind, humble, and grateful. When we do these things, we'll be rewarded with the comfort and peace God gives to those who trust Him completely and follow His path.

Would you like to experience God's comfort and abundance? Then don't look for shortcuts, and don't expect impulsivity or immaturity to bring happiness. Instead, determine to act and think like a mature, thoughtful, obedient adult. Then get ready to receive the rewards God bestows upon His children . . . who act like grown-ups.

God's plan for our guidance is for us to grow gradually in wisdom before we get to the crossroads.

Bill Hybels

Give Me Patience, Lord, Right Now!

We urge you, brethren, admonish the unruly, encourage the fainthearted, help the weak, be patient with everyone.
1 Thessalonians 5:14 NASB

He's known as the inventor of bifocals and the lightning rod, but one might also say that Benjamin Franklin was a co-inventor of America. He was one of our nation's most vocal founding fathers, one of its most successful publishers, and one of its most creative scientists. Yet Franklin observed, "Genius is nothing more than a greater aptitude for patience." This master of many disciplines understood that patience pays.

What was good for ol' Ben is good for you, too: patience pays powerful dividends, especially when it means being patient with the folks you encounter in everyday life. So today, when you're tempted to respond angrily to the delays and inconveniences that befall us all, be a little kinder–and a little more patient–than you have been in the past. When you do, God will smile . . . and so will your friends and neighbors.

The greatest and sublimest power
is often simple patience.
Horace Bushnell

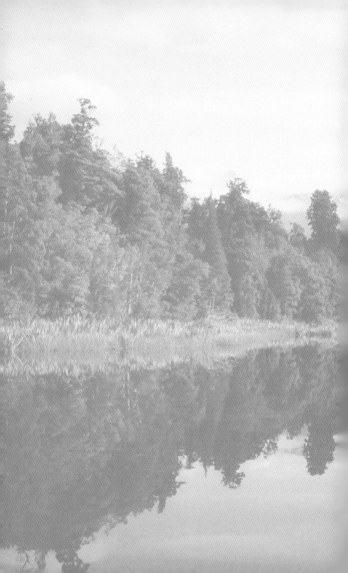

Faith That Moves Mountains

If you have faith as a mustard seed, you will say to this mountain, "Move from here to there," and it will move; and nothing will be impossible for you.

Matthew 17:20 NKJV

Are you a mountain mover whose faith is evident for all to see? Do you trust God, and do you believe He will help you do big things for Him?

Because we live in a demanding world, all of us have mountains to climb and mountains to move. Moving those mountains requires faith, and plenty of it.

God needs more people who are willing to move mountains for His glory and for His kingdom. But the Almighty walks with you, ready and willing to strengthen you. Accept His strength today. And remember—Jesus taught his disciples that if they had faith, they could move mountains. You can too . . . so with no further delay, let the mountain moving begin.

Only God can move mountains,
but faith and prayer can move God.

E. M. Bounds

Taking Time to Ask

He granted their request because they trusted in Him.
1 Chronicles 5:20 HCSB

Sometimes, amid the demands and frustrations of everyday life, we forget to slow down long enough to talk with God. Instead of turning our thoughts and prayers to Him, we rely on our own resources. Instead of praying for strength and courage, we seek to manufacture it within ourselves. Instead of asking God for guidance, we depend on our own limited wisdom. The results of such behaviors are unfortunate and, on occasion, can even be tragic.

Are you in need? Ask God to sustain you. Are you troubled? Take your worries to Him in prayer. Are you weary? Seek God's strength. In all things great and small, seek God's wisdom and His grace. He hears your prayers and He will answer. All you must do is ask.

When trials come your way–as inevitably they will–do not run away. Run to your God and Father.
Kay Arthur

Expect Success

May the Lord our God show us his approval and make our efforts successful. Yes, make our efforts successful!
Psalm 90:17 NLT

Neil Armstrong served as a U.S. Navy aviator in Korea and was a test pilot before he joined NASA as an astronaut. Then, as commander of *Apollo 11*, he took one small step that placed him forever in the history books—he was the first human to set foot on the moon. When questioned about his space flights, Neil Armstrong replied, "We planned for every negative contingency, but we expected success."

If you'd like to launch your life to new heights, take a hint from the first man on the moon: plan for the worst—but don't expect the worst. When it comes to your expectations, pray, have faith, and set your sights on success. Then, like Neil Armstrong, you can confidently shoot for the moon. An attitude of faith and optimism is a giant step forward, and when you trust God and work for success, He will bless your efforts.

You live up—or down—to your expectations.
Lou Holtz

A Life of Fulfillment

You, O God, have tested us; You have refined us as silver is refined. . . . We went through fire and through water; but You brought us out to rich fulfillment.

Psalm 66:10, 12 NKJV

How can we find genuine fulfillment? Is it by trusting the world's promises or by achieving success as the world defines it? Hardly. Real fulfillment starts and ends with God, not with the world. When we trust God's promises, seek God's will, and live in accordance with God's teachings, we will experience the true fulfillment that only He can offer.

Sometimes, amid the hustle and bustle of life, we can forfeit the gift of God's joy as we wrestle with the challenges of daily living. Yet God's Word is clear: spiritual abundance is available to all who seek it. Count yourself among that number. Seek first a personal, transforming relationship with your Creator, and then claim the joy, the fulfillment, and the spiritual riches that can and should be yours.

I'm fulfilled in what I do. . . . I never thought that a lot of money or fine clothes–the finer things of life–would make you happy. My concept of happiness is to be filled in a spiritual sense.

Coretta Scott King

God Is Love

God is love; and he that dwelleth in love dwelleth in God, and God in him.

1 John 4:16 KJV

The Bible tells us this great truth: God is love. It's a sweeping statement, a profoundly important description of what God is and how God works. His love is infinite, all-encompassing, and complete.

When we open our hearts to God's perfect love, we are touched by the Creator's hand, and thus we are transformed. When we trust our heavenly Father, we are rewarded for our faithfulness. When we honor God with our thoughts, our prayers, and our actions, He blesses us in surprising ways.

So today, even if you can only carve out a few quiet moments, offer sincere prayers of thanksgiving to your Creator. He loves you now and always. Open your heart to His presence and His love.

The life of faith is a daily exploration of the constant and countless ways in which God's grace and love are experienced.

Eugene Peterson

Deciding to Do It God's Way

Teach me Your way, O Lord; I will walk in Your truth.
Psalm 86:11 NKJV

Each of us faces thousands of small choices each day, choices that make up the fabric of daily life. When we align those choices with the instructions in God's Word, and when we align our lives with God's will, we'll receive His peace, His joy, and His comfort. But when we struggle against God's will for our lives—when we insist on doing things our way and not God's way—we'll reap a less bountiful harvest.

Today you'll face thousands of small decisions; as you do, use God's Word as your guide. And while you're at it, pay careful attention to the still, small voice of God whispering in your heart. In matters great and small, seek the will of God and trust Him. He will never lead you astray.

In the center of a hurricane there is absolute quiet and peace. There is no safer place than in the center of the will of God.
Corrie ten Boom

God's Timetable

Humble yourselves, therefore, under God's mighty hand, that he may lift you up in due time.
1 Peter 5:6 NIV

We know we should trust God's timing, yet we often find that hard to do. Why? Because we human beings are usually anxious for things to happen sooner rather than later. But God knows better.

God has created a world that unfolds according to His schedule, not ours. Thank goodness! We mortals might make a terrible mess of things, but God knows what He's doing. His plan doesn't always work out the way we think it should or in the time we think it should. But it's God's job to know the best way; our task is to wait patiently and never lose hope.

In the words of Elisabeth Elliot, "We must learn to move according to the timetable of the Timeless One, and to be at peace." That's advice worth following—for all time.

Grass that is here today and gone tomorrow does not require much time to mature. A big oak tree that lasts for generations requires much more time to grow and mature. God is concerned about your life through eternity. Allow Him to take all the time He needs to shape you for His purposes. Larger assignments will require longer periods of preparation.
Henry Blackaby

Wisdom and Perspective

Everyone who hears these words of mine
and puts them into practice is like a wise man
who built his house on the rock.
Matthew 7:24 NIV

Sometimes, amid the demands of daily life, it's easy to lose perspective. Life may feel out of balance, and the pressures of everyday living may seem overwhelming. What's needed is a fresh perspective, a restored sense of balance . . . and God's wisdom. If we call upon the Lord and seek to see the world through His eyes, He will give us guidance and perspective.

Where will you place your trust today? Will you trust in the wisdom of the world, the imperfect insights of fallible men and women, or will you place your faith in God's perfect wisdom? Where you choose to place your trust will greatly influence the quality and direction of your day—and of your life. So choose God. When you trust His wisdom and accept His love, you'll regain your perspective . . . and so much more.

God's plan for our guidance is for us to grow gradually in wisdom before we get to the crossroads.
Bill Hybels

Love That Lasts

Above all, [put on] love–the perfect bond of unity.

Colossians 3:14 HCSB

Genuine love requires patience and perseverance. Sometimes we're sorely tempted to treat love as if it were a sprint. But genuine love is always a marathon, and those who expect it to be otherwise will be disappointed.

Building lasting relationships requires a steadfast determination to endure and a willingness to persevere, even when times are tough. To see the power of perseverance, we need look no further than the life of Jesus Christ. He finished what He began, and so can we.

So the next time you're tempted to give up on a relationship, take a moment to reflect on how Jesus would respond. He is always faithful, always loving toward you. Ask Him to fill your heart with His love so that you can bless others with a love that lasts.

I have found the paradox,
that if you love until it hurts,
there can be no more hurt, only more love.

Mother Teresa

Really Trusting God

It is better to trust the Lord than to trust people.
It is better to trust the Lord than to trust princes.

Psalm 118:8–9 NCV

Talking about trusting God is easy; actually trusting Him is considerably harder. Genuine trust in God requires more than words; it requires a willingness to follow God's lead, a willingness to accept His providence, and a willingness to obey His commandments. These are not easy things to do.

Have you spent more time talking about Jesus than walking in His footsteps? If so, maybe it's time to have a little talk with God. Thankfully, whenever you're willing to talk with God, He's willing to listen. And the instant you decide to place Him squarely in the center of your life, He will respond to that decision with blessings that are too wonderful to predict and too numerous to count.

Do you seek a renewed sense of purpose for your life? Then don't just talk about trusting God; trust Him! Trust Him completely and without reservation. And then prepare yourself for a cascade of blessings from above.

God is God. He knows what he is doing.
When you can't trace his hand, trust his heart.

Max Lucado

Midcourse Corrections

The prudent see danger and take refuge,
but the simple keep going and suffer for it.
Proverbs 27:12 NIV

In our fast-paced world, it seems everyday life has become an exercise in managing change. Our circumstances change; our relationships change; our careers change; our bodies change. We grow older every day, as does the world around us. Thankfully, God does not change. He is eternal, and so are the truths found in His Word.

Are you facing one of life's midcourse corrections? Are you apprehensive about things in the future that you can neither see nor predict? If so, take comfort; you can place your faith, your trust, and your life in the hands of the One who does not change–your heavenly Father. He is the unmoving rock upon which you can build your life, this day and every day. When you do, you are secure.

When you come to a roadblock, take a detour.
Mary Kay Ash

The Simple Life

Whoever becomes simple and elemental again,
like this child, will rank high in God's kingdom.
Matthew 18:4 MSG

In our world, it seems simplicity is in short supply. Think for a moment about the complexity of your daily life and compare it with the lives of your ancestors. Certainly you are the beneficiary of many technological innovations, but those innovations come at a price; in all likelihood, your world is highly complex.

Unless you take firm control of your time and your life, you may become overwhelmed by an ever-increasing tidal wave of complexity. It can even threaten your happiness. But your heavenly Father understands the joy of living simply, with the trust and joy of a child. He wants you to know this way of living. So do yourself a favor: keep your life as simple as possible. When you do, and when you return to childlike faith in your Father, you'll discover the joy and comfort of the simple life.

I believe that a simple and unassuming manner
of life is best for everyone,
best both for the body and the mind.
Albert Einstein

Rest and Health

Rest in God alone, my soul, for my hope comes from Him.
Psalm 62:5 HCSB

God promises that when we come to Him, He will give us rest—but we must do our part. We must take the necessary steps to ensure that we get sufficient rest and that we take care of our bodies in other ways too.

Each of us bears a measure of responsibility for the general state of our own physical health. Certainly, various aspects of health are beyond our control: illness sometimes strikes even the most health-conscious men and women. But for most of us, physical fitness is a choice: it's the result of hundreds of small decisions that we make every day of our lives. If we make decisions that promote good health, our bodies respond. But if we fall into bad habits and undisciplined lifestyles, we suffer the consequences.

So today, treat your body as a priceless asset on loan from God. Take good care of yourself . . . you belong to Him.

You can't buy good health at the doctor's office—you've got to earn it for yourself.
Marie T. Freeman

Confidence Restored

I've told you all this so that trusting me, you will be unshakable and assured, deeply at peace. In this godless world you will continue to experience difficulties. But take heart! I've conquered the world.

John 16:33 MSG

Are you confident about your future, or do you live under a cloud of uncertainty and doubt? If you trust God's promises, you have every reason to live comfortably and confidently. Yet despite God's promises, and despite His blessings, you may, from time to time, find yourself tormented by doubts and negative emotions. When you do, step back and redirect your thoughts and your prayers.

Even the most optimistic men and women may be overcome by occasional bouts of fear and doubt. But even when you feel discouraged—or worse—remember that God is always faithful, and He is always with you. When you sincerely seek Him, He will comfort your heart, calm your fears, and restore your confidence.

As I have grown in faith and confidence, I have known more and more that my worth is based on the love of God.

Leslie Williams

The Rewards of Hard Work

Each will receive his own reward according to his own labor. . . . Each man's work will become evident.

1 Corinthians 3:8, 13 NASB

It would not be an overstatement to say that Thomas Edison revolutionized the world. He became, perhaps, America's most productive inventor despite the fact that his formal education was limited to a mere three months.

Edison patented the first practical lightbulb, the phonograph, motion-picture equipment, and more than a thousand other devices. When questioned about his success, he quipped, "Genius is one percent inspiration and ninety-nine percent perspiration."

Edison's success came not just from creative genius but from endless hours of good, old-fashioned, hard work. So the next time your life's journey feels a little uphill, remember Thomas Edison, and renew your energies. Keep working at your task, and you'll be one day closer to success.

I do not know anyone who has got to the top without hard work. That is the recipe.
It will not always get you to the top,
but should get you pretty near to it.

Margaret Thatcher

Defeating Depression

I have heard your prayer, I have seen your tears;
surely I will heal you.
2 Kings 20:5 NKJV

The sadness that accompanies any significant loss is inevitable. In time, sadness runs its course. Gradually it abates. Some days are light and happy, and some days feel like heavy weights on our hearts. When we face those dark days, how we respond is paramount. Will we allow ourselves to sink even deeper into sadness, or will we take steps to begin pulling out of that bog? We can bring light to the dark days of life by turning first to God, and then to trusted family members, friends, and medical professionals.

When we take those first steps, we can trust that God will be faithful, the clouds will eventually part, and the sun will shine once more upon our souls.

To win one's joy through struggle is better
than to yield to melancholy.
André Gide

Modern-Day Discipleship

He has showed you, O man, what is good.
And what does the Lord require of you?
To act justly and to love mercy
and to walk humbly with your God.
Micah 6:8 NIV

When Jesus addressed His disciples, He warned that each one must "take up his cross and follow me." In Jesus's day, prisoners were forced to carry their own crosses to the location where they would be crucified. Thus the message was clear: in order to follow Christ, the disciples must deny themselves and trust Him completely.

Nothing has changed since then.

If we sincerely want to be modern-day disciples of God's Son, then we must make Him the focus of our lives, not merely an afterthought.

Would you like to experience the peace, the joy, the comfort, and the contentment that come from being a disciple of the One from Galilee? Then find a way to pick up His cross and carry it. When you do, He will bless you . . . now and forever.

Discipleship is a decision to live by what I know about God, not by what I feel about him or myself or my neighbors.
Eugene Peterson

The Son of Encouragement

A cheerful look brings joy to the heart,
and good news gives health to the bones.
Proverbs 15:30 NIV

Barnabas, a man whose name meant "Son of Encouragement," was a leader in the early Christian church. He was known for his kindness and for his ability to encourage others. Because of Barnabas, many people heard about Jesus. Today, living in a difficult world, we should seek to imitate the "Son of Encouragement."

We imitate Barnabas when we speak kind words to our families and to our friends. We imitate Barnabas when our actions give credence to our beliefs. We imitate Barnabas when we are generous with our possessions and with our praise. We imitate Barnabas when we give hope to the hopeless and encouragement to the downtrodden.

Today, be like Barnabas: become a source of encouragement to those who cross your path. When you do, you can quite literally change the world—one person and one moment at a time.

God is still in the process of dispensing gifts,
and He uses ordinary individuals like us to develop those gifts in other people.
Howard Hendricks

The Importance of Family

Love one another earnestly from a pure heart.
1 Peter 1:22 HCSB

A loving family is a treasure from God. If you happen to be a member of a close-knit, supportive clan, offer a word of thanks to your heavenly Father. He has blessed you with one of His most precious earthy possessions. In response to God's gift, be sure to treat your family with love, respect, courtesy, and care.

We live in a competitive world, a place where earning a living can be difficult and demanding. As pressures build, we may focus so intently upon our careers (or other obligations) that we lose sight, at least temporarily, of perhaps less urgent but more important needs. We must never overlook our families. As we establish priorities for our days and our lives, we'll be wise to place God first . . . and family next.

As the family goes, so goes the nation
and so goes the whole world in which we live.
Pope John Paul II

Your Growing Faith

Let us stop going over the basic teachings about Christ again and again. Let us go on instead and become mature in our understanding.

Hebrews 6:1 NLT

Building and sustaining our faith is an ongoing process–and requires ongoing work. But the work of nourishing our faith can and should be joyful. The hours we invest in Bible study, prayer, meditation, and worship can be times of enrichment and celebration.

As we build our lives upon the foundation of faith, we will discover that the journey toward spiritual maturity lasts a lifetime. But it is a journey rich with blessing.

Are you willing to spend time each day with God? Are you willing to study His Word and apply it to your life? Determine to do those things today (and every day), because as a child of God, you're never fully grown. You can continue "growing up" every day of your life. And that's exactly what God wants you to do.

God is teaching me to become more and more "teachable": To keep evolving. To keep taking the risk of learning something new . . . or unlearning something old and off base.

Beth Moore

God's Surprising Plans

It is God who is at work in you,
both to will and to work for His good pleasure.
Philippians 2:13 NASB

His best-selling devotional book first saw print six years after his death in 1923. This man's name was Oswald Chambers, and the book was *My Utmost for His Highest*, a classic that remains popular today. But that devotional gem would never have seen publication had it not been for Gertrude Hobbs Chambers, who compiled the book from meticulous notes she had taken during her late husband's sermons and lectures.

In Jeremiah 29:11 God says, "I know what I am planning for you. . . . I will give you hope and a good future" (NCV). The story of Oswald Chambers teaches us that God can use us not just during our lifetimes; He may continue to use us long after we've gone on to our heavenly reward.

So today, trust God, get busy, and leave the rest to the heavenly Father whose plans for your life are far greater than you can imagine.

Never place a period where
God has placed a comma.
Mother Teresa

First Things First

Pay careful attention, then, to how you walk.
Ephesians 5:15 HCSB

On our daily to-do list, all items are not equal: certain tasks are extremely important, while others are not. So it's imperative that we prioritize our daily activities and give attention to each task in the approximate order of its importance.

The principle of doing first things first is simple in theory but more complicated in practice. Well-meaning family, friends, and coworkers have a way of making unexpected demands on our time. Add to that each day's share of minor emergencies; these trival matters tend to draw our attention away from more important ones. On paper, prioritizing is simple, but to act upon those priorities in the real world requires maturity, patience, and determination.

If you don't prioritize your day, life will do the job for you. So your choice is simple: prioritize or be prioritized. It's a choice that will set the tone for—and affect the quality of—your life.

Things which matter most must never be
at the mercy of things which matter least.
Goethe

God's Guidance and Your Path

Trust in the Lord with all your heart; do not depend on your own understanding. Seek his will in all you do, and he will show you which path to take.
Proverbs 3:5–6 NLT

Proverbs 3:5–6 makes this promise: if you acknowledge God's sovereignty over every aspect of your life, He will guide your path. As you prayerfully consider the path God wants you to take, here are some other things you can do to keep on the right path: Study God's Word and be ever watchful for His signs. Associate with faith-filled, optimistic friends who will encourage your spiritual growth. Listen carefully to that still, small voice that speaks to you in the quiet moments of your daily devotional time. And be patient.

Your heavenly Father may not always reveal Himself as quickly as you'd like, but rest assured that He wants to use you in wonderful, unexpected ways. Your challenge is to watch, to listen, to learn, and to follow.

Only by walking with God can we hope to find the path that leads to life.
John Eldredge

Keep Possessions in Perspective

A man's life does not consist in the abundance of his possessions.
Luke 12:15 NIV

All too often we focus our thoughts and energies on the accumulation of earthly treasures, leaving precious little time to accumulate the only treasures that really matter—the spiritual kind. Our material possessions have the potential to do great good depending upon how we use them. But if we allow the things we own to own us, we may pay dearly for our misplaced priorities.

Much of society focuses intently on material possessions; however, God's Word teaches us that money matters little when compared to the spiritual gifts the Creator offers to those who put Him first in their lives. So today, keep your possessions in perspective. Remember that God should come first and everything else next. When you give God His rightful place in your heart, you'll have a clearer vision of the things that really matter. Then you can joyfully thank your heavenly Father for the abundant spiritual blessings He sends your way.

True contentment comes from godliness in the heart, not from wealth in the hand.
Warren Wiersbe

He Renews Our Strength

Do you not know? Have you not heard? The Everlasting God, the Lord, the Creator of the ends of the earth does not become weary or tired. His understanding is inscrutable. He gives strength to the weary, and to him who lacks might He increases power.

Isaiah 40:28–29 NASB

When we lift our hearts and prayers to God, He renews our strength. Are you almost too weary to lift your head? Then bow it. Offer your concerns and your fears to your Father in heaven. He is always at your side, offering you His love and His strength.

Are you troubled or anxious? Take your anxieties to God in prayer. Are you weak or worried? Delve deeply into God's Word. Bask in His presence in the quiet moments of your day.

Are you spiritually exhausted? Call upon your Creator to renew your spirit and your life. God will never let you down. He will always lift you up if you go to Him. When you ask for strength, He answers—so why not ask Him now?

Troubles we bear trustfully can bring us a fresh vision of God and a new outlook on life, an outlook of peace and hope.

Billy Graham

The Seeds of Happiness

They are blessed whose thoughts are pure,
for they will see God.
Matthew 5:8 NCV

Her first husband, a man named Daniel Park Custis, had died. Young Martha Custis was left to raise her two surviving children alone. But two years later she remarried, this time to a man named George Washington, and later became America's first First Lady.

Despite the tragedies in her life, Martha remained optimistic. She said, "We carry the seeds of happiness with us wherever we go." And she was right.

The next time you're feeling blue, remember that wherever you go, you carry seeds of happiness—the potential to be happy yourself and the potential to share that happiness with others. Realizing that potential is up to you. The first step is to turn your thoughts and your heart toward God. He will fill your heart with joy. Then, take the seeds of happiness . . . and plant them!

Happiness is a matter of your own doing.
You can be happy, or you can be unhappy.
It's just according to the way you look at things.
Walt Disney

Be Patient with Yourself

Patience is better than pride.
Ecclesiastes 7:8 NLT

Being patient with other people can be difficult. But sometimes we find it even more difficult to be patient with ourselves. We have high expectations and lofty goals. We want to accomplish things now, not later. We want our lives to unfold according to our plans and timing. But what about God's plan and timing? Actually, God's timetable supercedes our own, whether we like it or not.

Patience and wisdom are traveling companions. And for most of us, learning the art of patience means learning how to be patient not only with other people, but also with ourselves.

So today, practice understanding and patience with everybody–beginning with the person in the mirror.

Have patience with all things, but chiefly have patience with yourself. Do not lose courage in considering your own imperfections,
but instantly set about remedying them–
every day begin the task anew.
Saint Francis de Sales

Terminating the Tantrum

Bad temper is contagious–don't get infected.

Proverbs 22:25 MSG

Temper tantrums are usually unproductive, unattractive, unforgettable, unnecessary, and uncomfortable. Perhaps that's why Proverbs 16:32 says, "Controlling your temper is better than capturing a city" (NCV).

If you've allowed anger to become a regular visitor at your house, ask God for wisdom, for patience, and for a heart that is so filled with love and forgiveness that it has no room for bitterness. Bitterness is emotional poison and crossness is corrosive. If you desire emotional peace and spiritual comfort, one important step is finding ways to control your temper.

God will help you terminate tantrums if you ask Him, so why not ask Him today? It'll be better than capturing a city–you may just recapture the goodwill and affection of those around you.

Keep cool; anger is not an argument.

Daniel Webster

The Direction of Your Thoughts

My cup runs over. Surely goodness and mercy shall follow me all the days of my life; and I will dwell in the house of the Lord forever.

Psalm 23:5–6 NKJV

God has given you not only the ability to think, but also the ability to control the direction of your thoughts. So how will you direct your thoughts today? Will you focus on your opportunities, your blessings, and your hopes for the future?

The quality of your thought life will help determine the quality of the rest of your life—so guard your thoughts accordingly. The next time you find yourself dwelling on something negative, refocus your attention on things positive. And the next time you're tempted to waste valuable time worrying or complaining, resist that temptation with all your might. Turn your thoughts to God and to the bountiful blessings of goodness and mercy He has bestowed on your life. You'll see that your cup's running over with good things.

The life of strain is difficult.
The life of inner peace—a life that comes from a positive attitude—is the easiest type of existence.

Norman Vincent Peale

Don't Dread Tomorrow

Do not worry about tomorrow, for tomorrow will worry about itself. Each day has enough trouble of its own.
Matthew 6:34 NIV

Long before "Dear Abby" or Ann Landers, a woman named Dorothy Dix wrote a newspaper column that offered advice to readers from the Atlantic to the Pacific. Dix was a syndicated columnist who, in the late 1930s, appeared in newspapers with a combined circulation of 60 million copies per day.

Dorothy was a practical woman who had simple yet profound advice for life. She said, "I have learned to live each day as it comes, and not to borrow trouble by dreading tomorrow. It is the dark menace of the future that makes cowards of us."

If dreading some distant possibility is draining your time and energy, plug that drain with faith. No one ever changed the future by dreading it, so instead of worrying, simply do your best and have faith—God will take care of tomorrow. When you trust Him, you'll find that you can take comfort knowing He'll take care of everything.

Don't take tomorrow to bed with you.
Norman Vincent Peale

Making a Masterpiece

Give your entire attention to what God is doing right now, and don't get worked up about what may or may not happen tomorrow. God will help you deal with whatever hard things come up when the time comes.

Matthew 6:34 MSG

Coach John Wooden was inducted into the Basketball Hall of Fame twice—first as a player and then as a coach. As a player, he was a member of Purdue's 1932 national championship team. He then became a successful college coach. During his storied coaching career, he led UCLA to ten national championships, a record that remains unbroken. Coach Wooden's advice for life was straightforward: "Make each day your masterpiece."

Yesterday is in the past, and tomorrow is never guaranteed. That leaves one day, this one, in which you can create a work of art with your life. So follow the coach's advice and give this day the best you have to offer. When you do that, each day will become not just an individual masterpiece, but a part of the beautiful mosaic God is making of your life.

The past, the present and the future are really one: they are today.

Harriet Beecher Stowe

June

Compassionate Servants

All of you be of one mind, having compassion for one another; love as brothers, be tenderhearted, be courteous.
1 Peter 3:8 NKJV

God's Word instructs us to be compassionate, generous servants to those who need our support. As men and women who have been richly blessed by the Creator, we should share our gifts, our possessions, our talents, and our hopes with the world.

Concentration-camp survivor Corrie ten Boom correctly observed, "The measure of a life, after all, is not its duration, but its donation." These words remind us that the quality of our lives is determined not by what we're able to get from others, but by what we are able to share with others.

The thread of compassion is woven into the fabric of Jesus's teachings. And like the One from Galilee, we, too, should be zealous in caring for others. We should serve with smiles on our faces and empathy in our hearts. And make no mistake: when we bless others, we, too, will be blessed . . . *richly* blessed.

Our Lord worked with people as they were,
and He was patient–not tolerant of sin,
but compassionate.
Vance Havner

The Power of Words

Watch the way you talk.
Let nothing foul or dirty come out of your mouth.
Say only what helps, each word a gift.
Ephesians 4:29 MSG

The words we speak have the power to do great good or great harm. If we speak words of encouragement and hope, we can lift others up. When we do, the effect on us is uplifting too.

Sometimes, when we already feel uplifted and secure, we find it easy to speak kind words. But other times, when we're discouraged or exhausted, we can scarcely summon the energy to pick up our own spirits, much less anyone else's. Yet God wants us to speak words of kindness, wisdom, and truth–no matter our circumstances, no matter our emotions. When we do, we share a priceless gift with the world, and we give glory to God.

Today, try to make your every word a gift. You'll discover that kindness is like honey: it's hard to spread it around without getting a little bit on yourself.

How many people stop because so few say, "Go!"
Charles Swindoll

Are You Enthusiastic?

Those who hope in the Lord will renew their strength. They will soar on wings like eagles; they will run and not grow weary, they will walk and not be faint.

Isaiah 40:31 NIV

Are you enthusiastic about your life and your faith? Are you genuinely excited about the upcoming day, the upcoming week, and the upcoming year? Are you optimistic about your life and your future?

If your zest for life has waned, now is the time to redirect your efforts and recharge your spiritual batteries. And that means taking a look at your priorities (to be sure you're putting God first) and counting your blessings (instead of your troubles).

Nothing is more important than your wholehearted commitment to your Creator. Faith should never be an afterthought; it should be your top priority, your most prized possession, and your deepest passion. When you become enthusiastic about your faith, you'll become enthusiastic about your life too. And then you'll feel the renewed energy and strength only God can give.

Your enthusiasm will be infectious, stimulating, and attractive to others. They will love you for it. They will go for you and with you.

Norman Vincent Peale

Temporary Setbacks

No matter how many times you trip them up, God-loyal people don't stay down long; soon they're up on their feet, while the wicked end up flat on their faces.

Proverbs 24:16 MSG

The occasional disappointments and failures in life are inevitable. Such setbacks are simply the price we occasionally pay for our willingness to take risks as we follow our dreams. But even when we encounter bitter disappointments, we must never lose faith.

When we encounter the difficulties of life that are sure to come, God stands ready to help us. Our responsibility, of course, is to ask Him for help. When we call upon Him in heartfelt prayer, He will answer—in His own time and according to His own plan—and He will heal our hearts when we hurt. And while we're waiting for God's plans to unfold and for His healing touch to restore us, we can be comforted in the knowledge that our Creator can overcome any obstacle, even if we cannot.

As long as a person keeps his faith in God and in himself, nothing can permanently defeat him.

Wilferd Peterson

An Awesome God

The fear of the Lord is a fountain of life.
Proverbs 14:27 NIV

God's hand shapes the universe—and it shapes our lives. The Creator maintains absolute sovereignty over His creation, and His power is beyond our comprehension. If we are wise, we'll develop a healthy respect for God and for His awesome power.

The Bible tells us that the fear of the Lord is the beginning of wisdom (Proverbs 1:7). But a healthy fear of the Lord also means the death of every other fear—because we sense and trust God's immense power to take care of us.

So today, as you face the sometimes scary realities of everyday life, instead of focusing on your fears, cultivate a reverent "fear" of God. Only then can your spiritual education—and your faith—be complete. Once you acknowledge God's power over everything, including you, you will have acquired the most important wisdom of all.

It is not possible that mortal men should be thoroughly conscious of the divine presence without being filled with awe.
C. H. Spurgeon

Recouping Your Losses

Misfortune pursues the sinner,
but prosperity is the reward of the righteous.
Proverbs 13:21 NIV

Have you ever committed a big-time blunder, a monumental mistake, or a super-sized slip up? If so, welcome to a very large club! Everybody makes mistakes from time to time. That probably wasn't your first, and it likely won't be your last.

When we take missteps in life, the best thing to do is to correct them, learn from them, and pray for the wisdom not to repeat them. When we take those positive steps, our mistakes become lessons and our lives become adventures in growth, not stagnation.

So here's today's big question: Have you used your mistakes as stumbling blocks or as stepping-stones? The way you respond to those incidents will have a lot to do with how quickly you regain your confidence . . . and how wisely you plan your next stage of life's journey.

[When you blunder,] blunder forward.
Thomas Edison

Blessed by Worship

Happy are those who hear the joyful call to worship,
for they will walk in the light of your presence, Lord.
Psalm 89:15 NLT

We should worship God in our hearts every day, but we should also worship in our churches, with fellow believers. When we do so, we'll discover the joys and the comfort that result from fellowship with friends and family members.

We live in a world that is teeming with temptations and distractions—a world where vice and virtue are locked in constant battle over our minds, our hearts, our souls, and our communities. But we play a part in the battle too. We must try to avoid the pitfalls of modern-day life and focus, instead, on the unchanging principles of God's Word. One way we remain faithful to our Creator is through the practice of regular, purposeful worship—in our churches and with our families. When we worship the Father faithfully and fervently, we will always be blessed.

Only participation in the full life of a local church builds spiritual muscle.

Rick Warren

God Can Handle It

Do not be afraid or discouraged, for the Lord will personally go ahead of you. He will be with you; he will neither fail you nor abandon you.

Deuteronomy 31:8 NLT

Life can be difficult and discouraging at times. During our darkest moments, God offers us strength and courage if we turn our hearts and our prayers to Him.

As children of God, we have every reason to live courageously. After all, God loves us and has promised to be with us. But sometimes, because we are imperfect human beings who possess imperfect faith, we fall prey to fear and doubt.

The next time you find your courage stretched to the limit, remember that your heavenly Father is as near as your next breath. He is your shield and your strength; He is your protector and your deliverer. Call upon Him in your hour of need, and be comforted. Whatever your challenge, whatever your trouble, God can handle it . . . and He will!

Walk boldly and wisely.
There is a hand above that will help thee on.

Philip James Bailey

Letting God Decide

A man's heart plans his way,
but the Lord directs his steps.
Proverbs 16:9 NKJV

The world will often lead you astray, but God never will. His counsel is always wise, always the best course to take . . . because it leads you to Him. Are you facing a difficult decision, a troubling circumstance, or a powerful temptation? If so, it's time to step back, stop focusing on the world, and focus instead on the will of your Father in heaven.

Everyday living is an exercise in decision making. Today and every day, you must make choices: choices about what you will do, what you will worship, and how you will think. When in doubt, make choices that you sincerely believe will bring you to a closer relationship with God. And if you're uncertain of your next step, pray about it. When you do, God will answer–and His will always be the right answers for you.

God always gives His best to those who
leave the choice with Him.
Jim Elliot

Dealing with Difficult People

You have heard that it was said,
"Love your neighbor and hate your enemy." But I tell you:
Love your enemies and pray for those who persecute you,
that you may be sons of your Father in heaven.
Matthew 5:43–45 NIV

Sometimes people can be discourteous and cruel. Sometimes people can be unfair, unkind, and unappreciative. Sometimes people get angry and frustrated. So what's a person to do? God's answer is straightforward: forgive, pray, and love. In Luke 6:37 Jesus said, "Do not judge, and you will not be judged. Do not condemn, and you will not be condemned. Forgive, and you will be forgiven" (HCSB).

Today and every day, be quick to forgive others for their shortcomings. And when other people misbehave (as they most certainly will from time to time), don't pay too much attention. Just forgive those people as quickly as you can, remembering your own shortcomings and bad days; then pray for them and show kindness whenever you can. After all, that's what Jesus did for you.

A keen sense of humor helps us to overlook the unbecoming,
understand the unconventional, tolerate the unpleasant,
overcome the unexpected, and outlast the unbearable.
Billy Graham

The Need for Self-Discipline

Do you not know that those who run in a race all run, but only one receives the prize? Run in such a way that you may win. Everyone who competes in the games exercises self-control in all things.

1 Corinthians 9:24–25 NASB

God's Word tells us clearly that we must exercise self-discipline in all matters. Self-discipline is not simply a proven way to get ahead; it's also an integral part of God's plan for our lives. If we genuinely seek to be faithful stewards of our time, our talents, and our resources, we must adopt a disciplined approach to life. Otherwise, our talents will be wasted and our resources squandered.

The good news is, hard work and perseverance result in some of the greatest rewards we can experience. May we, as disciplined believers, be willing to work for the rewards—spiritual as well as material—we so earnestly desire.

God provides the ingredients for our daily bread
but expects us to do the baking.
With our own hands!

Barbara Johnson

Always Forgiving

Peter came to him and asked, "Lord, how often should I forgive someone who sins against me? Seven times?" "No, not seven times," Jesus replied, "but seventy times seven!

Matthew 18:21–22 NLT

How often should we forgive other people? More times than we can count. That's a tall order, but we must remember that it's an order from God. And even when God asks us to do something difficult, we can be assured that it's for our good—that He will help us to obey Him.

In God's curriculum, forgiveness isn't optional; it's a required course. That doesn't mean it's easy. Forgiving people who have hurt us deeply is one of the hardest things to do. But if we fail to forgive others, we hurt ourselves most of all. When our hearts are filled with bitterness, there's no room left for love.

Today, search your heart: note all the people you haven't yet forgiven . . . and forgive them. No matter how long you've held that grudge, it's always the right time—and it's never too late—to let it go.

Having forgiven, I am liberated.

Father Lawrence Jenco

Today's Journey

*Live full lives, full in the fullness of God. God can do anything, you know–far more than you could ever imagine or guess or request in your wildest dreams!
He does it not by pushing us around but by working within us, his Spirit deeply and gently within us.*
Ephesians 3:19–20 MSG

This day, like every other, is full of opportunities, challenges, and choices. But no choice you make is more important than the choice you make concerning God. Today, you will either place Him at the center of your life . . . or not. And the consequences of that choice are both temporal and eternal.

Sometimes, without our even realizing, we gradually drift from the One we need most. Thankfully, God never drifts away from us. He remains always present, always steadfast, always loving.

As you begin this day, place God first in your thoughts, on your lips, and in your heart. And then, with the Creator of the universe as your guide and companion, you can face today's journey with courage.

You cannot be the person God meant you to be, and you cannot live the life He meant you to live, unless you live from the heart.
John Eldredge

The Treasure Hunt

Where your treasure is, there your heart will be also.
Luke 12:34 NKJV

All of mankind is engaged in a colossal, worldwide treasure hunt. Some people seek treasure in earthly sources, such as material wealth or public acclaim; others seek God's treasures by making Him the cornerstone of their lives.

What kind of treasure hunter are you? Are you so caught up in the demands of everyday living that you sometimes allow the search for worldly treasures to become your primary focus? If so, it's time to think again about what you value, and why. All the items on your daily to-do list are not of the same import. That's why you must put first things first by placing God in His rightful place: first place.

The world's treasures are difficult to find and difficult to keep; God's treasures are available to all, and they are everlasting. Which treasures will you seek?

It's sobering to contemplate how much time, effort, sacrifice, compromise, and attention we give to acquiring and increasing our supply of something that is totally insignificant in eternity.

Anne Graham Lotz

Optimism Pays

This hope we have as an anchor of the soul,
a hope both sure and steadfast.
Hebrews 6:19 NASB

In 1919, Conrad Hilton paid $5,000 for a small Texas hotel and began acquiring more properties. Over the years, his name became synonymous with quality and service. He even purchased New York's famed Waldorf-Astoria Hotel and made it the crown jewel in his chain. Hilton's advice for life was as expansive as Texas. He said, "Think big. Act big. Dream big."

If you've been plagued by pessimism and doubt, reconsider that way of thinking, and return to an attitude of faith and optimism. Good things do happen to good people, but the best things are usually reserved for those who expect the best and plan for it. So start dreaming in Technicolor. Think optimistically about your world and your life. Since dreams often do come true, you might as well make your dreams Texas sized. There's no limit to what God can do!

I am an optimist.
It does not seem too much use being anything else.
Winston Churchill

Pleasing God

Cheerfully pleasing God is the main thing,
and that's what we aim to do, regardless of our conditions.
2 Corinthians 5:9 MSG

When God made you, He equipped you with an array of talents and abilities that are uniquely yours. It's up to you to develop those talents and to use them, but sometimes the world will discourage you. At times, society will attempt to pigeonhole you, to standardize you, to make you fit into a particular mold. Sometimes you may become so wrapped up in meeting those expectations that you fail to focus on God's expectations. But this is a mistake of major proportions—don't make it.

Whom will you try to please today, God or man? Your primary obligation is not to please imperfect men and women. Your obligation is to strive diligently to meet the expectations of an all-knowing and perfect God. Trust Him always. Love Him always. Praise Him always. And seek to please Him. Always.

Don't be addicted to approval. Follow your heart. Do
what you believe God is telling you to do,
and stand firm in Him and Him alone.
Joyce Meyer

Community Life

Regarding life together and getting along with each other, you don't need me to tell you what to do. You're God-taught in these matters. Just love one another!

1 Thessalonians 4:9 MSG

As we travel along life's road, we build lifelong relationships with a small, dear circle of family and friends. And how best do we establish and maintain these relationships? For starters, by following the instructions in God's Word.

Healthy relationships are built upon honesty, compassion, responsible behavior, trust, and faith. Healthy relationships are built upon the Golden Rule. Healthy relationships are built upon sharing and caring. All of these principles are found time and time again in God's Word. When we read the Bible and follow its instruction, we enrich our own lives and the lives of those who are closest to us—and God smiles down upon us and our loved ones as we live together in a community of faith.

Horizontal relationships—relationships between people—are crippled at the outset unless the vertical relationship—the relationship between each person and God—is in place.

Ed Young

Critical of Yourself?

You made all the delicate, inner parts of my body
and knit me together in my mother's womb.
Thank you for making me so wonderfully complex!
Your workmanship is marvelous.
Psalm 139:13–14 NLT

Are you your own worst critic? Are you constantly trying to transform yourself into a person who meets others' expectations? If so, maybe it's time to be a little more understanding of the person you see when you look in the mirror.

Millions of words have been written about various ways to improve self-image and increase self-esteem. Yet maintaining a healthy self-image is really a matter of doing three things: (1) obeying God; (2) having faith; and (3) finding a purpose for your life that pleases your Creator and yourself.

So the next time you look in the mirror and see only flaws and failures, lighten up. God created you, and God only does good things. It's fine to want to be your best, but remember that God accepts you and loves you–faults and all. There's no better comfort.

May God help us to express and define
ourselves in our one-of-a-kind way.
Luci Swindoll

The Answer to Adversity

God is our refuge and strength,
a very present help in trouble.
Psalm 46:1 NKJV

From time to time, all of us must endure discouragement and defeat. We sometimes experience life-changing losses that leave us reeling. But when we do, God stands ready to help. When we are troubled, we can call upon God and in His perfect time and perfect way, He will heal us.

Are you anxious? Take those anxieties to God. Are you troubled? Take your troubles to Him. Does your world seem to be falling down around you? Seek protection from the One who cannot be moved. When you feel weak, give your troubles to God: He is strong. The same Being who created the universe will comfort and heal you—the answer to adversity is simply to ask.

When God is going to do a wonderful thing,
He begins with a difficulty.
When He is going to do a very wonderful thing,
he begins with an impossibility.
Charles Inwood

Opportunities Abound

I can do everything through him who gives me strength.

Philippians 4:13 NIV

Paradoxically, to make your dream come true, you have to stay awake and alert. That means keeping your eyes (and mind) open for new opportunities.

Whether you realize it or not, opportunities are whirling around you like stars crossing the night sky—beautiful to observe and too numerous to count. Yet we can get so preoccupied with the daily grind that we don't lift our eyes to the heavens to notice.

Today, take time to step back from the challenges of daily living. Lift your eyes toward heaven, and focus your thoughts on two things—on God and on the opportunities He has placed before you. If you let Him, He will lead you in the direction of those opportunities. So watch carefully, pray fervently, and then act accordingly.

With the right attitude and a willingness to pay the price, almost anyone can pursue nearly any opportunity and achieve it.

John Maxwell

Living in an Anxious World

Be anxious for nothing, but in everything by prayer and supplication, with thanksgiving, let your requests be made known to God.

Philippians 4:6 NKJV

We live in a world that often breeds anxiety and fear. When we come face-to-face with tough times, it's easy to fall into discouragement, doubt, or depression. But our Father in heaven has promised that we may lead lives of assurance, not anxiety. In fact, His Word instructs us to "be anxious for nothing." But how can we put our fears to rest? By taking those fears to God and leaving them there.

As you face the challenges of daily life, don't become anxious, troubled, discouraged, or fearful. Instead, turn every one of your concerns over to your heavenly Father. The same God who created the universe will comfort you if you ask Him . . . so ask Him and trust Him. And then watch in amazement as your anxieties melt into the warmth and comfort of His loving embrace.

Worry is interest paid on trouble before it is due.

William Ralph Inge

A Fresh Start

Do not remember the former things, nor consider the things of old. Behold, I will do a new thing.
Isaiah 43:18–19 NKJV

Each new day offers countless opportunities to celebrate life, to serve God, and to care for His children. But each day also offers opportunities to be hijacked by life's various complications and distractions. Thankfully, we are free to seek God's guidance whenever we choose. And whenever we ask Him to renew our strength and guide our steps, He will do so.

If you'd like to change some aspect of your life, consider this day a new beginning. Consider it a fresh start, a renewed opportunity to build a better life as you serve your Creator with willing hands and a loving heart. Ask God to renew your sense of purpose as He guides your steps. When you ask, He will answer.

This day is a glorious opportunity. Seize that opportunity while you can.

Every day we live is a priceless gift of God, loaded with possibilities to learn something new, to gain fresh insights.
Dale Evans Rogers

Smiles and More Smiles

What a relief to see your friendly smile.
It is like seeing the face of God!
Genesis 33:10 NLT

Life should never be taken for granted. Each day is a priceless gift from God and should be treated as such.

Hannah Whitall Smith observed, "How changed our lives would be if we could only fly through the days on wings of surrender and trust!" And Clement of Alexandria noted, "All our life is a celebration for us; we are convinced, in fact, that God is always everywhere. We sing while we work . . . we pray while we carry out all life's other occupations." Their words remind us that this day is God's creation, a gift to be treasured and savored.

Today, let us celebrate life with smiles on our faces and kind words on our lips. After all, this is God's day, and He has given us clear instructions for its use. We are commanded to rejoice and be glad. So let the celebration begin!

The men whom I have seen succeed best
in life always have been cheerful and hopeful men who
went about their business with
a smile on their faces.
Charles Kingsley

Be a Worshiper

Worship the Lord your God, and serve only Him.
Matthew 4:10 HCSB

God has a wonderful plan for your life, and an important part of that plan includes worship. We should never deceive ourselves: every life is based upon some form of worship. The question is not whether we worship but what we worship.

Some of us choose to worship God. The result is a plentiful harvest of joy, peace, and comfort. Others distance themselves from God by foolishly worshipping earthly possessions and personal gratification. But that will yield only sorrow in the end.

Have you welcomed God into your heart? Then worship Him today and every day. Worship Him with sincerity and thanksgiving. Worship Him early and often. Worship Him with your thoughts, your actions, your prayers, and your praise. Then prepare yourself for the spiritual gifts that always flow to people (like you) who put God first.

It's the definition of worship: A hungry heart finding the Father's feast. A searching soul finding the Father's face. A wandering pilgrim spotting the Father's house. Finding God. Finding God seeking us. This is worship. This is a worshiper.

Max Lucado

Recognizing Your Blessings

Bless the Lord, O my soul, and forget not all his benefits.
Psalm 103:2 KJV

This Yazoo City, Mississippi, feed salesman became a country comedian and spent more than twenty-five joyous years on the Grand Ole Opry. Howard Gerald "Jerry" Clower never told a joke you couldn't repeat in church, yet he sold millions of comedy records to adoring fans. Clower once said, "Lord, my cup runneth over and slosheth into the saucer."

Most of us are similar to Jerry in that we have more blessings than we can count. But sometimes we forget to even try to count them.

Today, slow down and take inventory of the benefits you've received from your heavenly Father. And then add this to your list of blessings–the ability to recognize those blessings and to know the God who bestows them. That truly is the greatest blessing.

Don't have anything to be thankful for?
Check your pulse!
Church sign

A Better World

Let us not grow weary while doing good, for in due season we shall reap if we do not lose heart.

Galatians 6:9 NKJV

Would you like to make the world a better place and feel better about yourself at the same time? If so, you can take a step in that direction by simply practicing the Golden Rule.

God's Word teaches us to treat other people with respect, with kindness, with courtesy, and with love. When we do, we make other people happy, we make God happy, and we feel better about ourselves. Everybody wins.

So if you're wondering how to make the world—starting with your little corner of it—a happier, healthier, more comforting place, start by doing something good for someone, showing some kindness, or offering some words of comfort. Your good deeds will come back around to comfort you as well.

Anything done for another is done for oneself.

Pope John Paul II

A God-Made Man

Respecting the Lord and not being proud will bring you wealth, honor, and life.

Proverbs 22:4 NCV

You've likely heard the phrase on countless occasions: "He's a self-made man." In truth, none of us are self-made. We all owe countless debts that we can never repay. Our first debt is to our Father in heaven—who has given us everything we are, everything we enjoy, and everything we ever will be—and to His Son, who sacrificed His own life on a cross so that we can be reconciled to God. We're also indebted to ancestors, parents, teachers, friends, spouses, family members, and coworkers . . . the list of those who've contributed to our lives in one way or another seems almost endless.

Most of us, if we're honest, are willing to stick out our chests and say, "Look at me; I did that!" But in our better moments, in the quiet moments when we search the depths of our own hearts, we know better. Whatever "it" is, God did that. And He deserves the credit.

Humility is not thinking less of yourself,
it's thinking of yourself less.

Rick Warren

Good Order

God hasn't invited us into a disorderly,
unkempt life but into something holy and beautiful—
as beautiful on the inside as the outside.
1 Thessalonians 4:7 MSG

If there's a secret to effective work, it may be organization: too much clutter hinders effectiveness. The more disorder in your life, the greater difficulty you'll have in accomplishing your goals. But when you introduce order into your daily affairs, you'll begin reaping surprising dividends.

No one can organize your life but you. It's up to you to invest the time and energy required to arrange your workplace and your home in an orderly fashion. So clean out that closet. Clear off that desk. Handle a piece of paper one time and be done with it. Keep an accurate daily calendar and keep your appointments. Spending even a little time each day organizing your tasks is well worth the effort.

Disorganization invites frustration, but good order is good for the soul.

Order means light and peace, inward liberty
and free command over one's self; order is power.
Henri Frédéric Amiel

Beyond Negativity

Don't pick on people, jump on their failures, criticize their faults–unless, of course, you want the same treatment. Don't condemn those who are down; that hardness can boomerang. Be easy on people; you'll find life a lot easier.

Luke 6:37 MSG

From experience, we know that it's easier to criticize than to correct. And we know it's easier to find faults than solutions. Yet the urge to criticize others remains a powerful temptation for most of us. As faith-filled believers, however, we should endeavor to break the twin habits of negative thinking and critical speech.

Negativity is highly contagious: we give it to others who, in turn, give it back to us. But this cycle can be broken by positive thoughts, heartfelt prayers, and encouraging words. As thoughtful servants of a loving God, we can use the transforming power of God's love to break the chains of negativity. Today, break those chains by showing kindness and offering comfort rather than criticism.

It takes less sense to criticize than to do anything else.

Sam Jones

Finding Encouragement

Be strong and courageous. Do not be terrified; do not be discouraged, for the Lord your God will be with you wherever you go.

Joshua 1:9 NIV

God offers us the strength to meet our challenges, and He offers us hope for the future. One way He communicates His message of hope is through the words of encouraging friends and family members.

Hope is something that must be nurtured if it is to grow. If we associate with hope-filled, positive people, their enthusiasm will have a tendency to buoy our spirits as well. But if we find ourselves spending too much time in the company of naysayers and cynics, our thoughts—like theirs—will tend toward pessimism.

Are you a hopeful, optimistic person who believes God has good plans for you? You can be assured that He does. Do you associate with those who understand God's loving nature? If so, you know just where to find encouragement—in your heavenly Father and with your spiritual brothers and sisters.

Overcoming discouragement is simply a matter of taking away the DIS and adding the EN.

Barbara Johnson

July

God's Big Plans for You

With God's power working in us, God can do much, much more than anything we can ask or imagine.
Ephesians 3:20 NCV

Are you willing to entertain the possibility that God has big plans in store for you? Your heavenly Father wants only the best for you, and He can do wonderful things in and through you. Yet sometimes, especially if you've recently experienced a deep disappointment, you may find it difficult to envision a brighter future for yourself and your family. If you're struggling in this way, perhaps it's time to take a second look at God's capabilities . . . and your God-given talents.

Your heavenly Father created you with unique gifts and abilities—perhaps some of them as yet untapped. Your job is to tap into them, and into God's strength. When you do, you'll begin to feel an increasing sense of faith and confidence and a brighter outlook on the future.

So even if you're going through difficult days now, don't abandon your dreams. Instead, trust that God is preparing you for greater things. His power is at work in you.

You cannot out-dream God.
John Eldredge

Success and Service

Prepare your minds for service and have self-control.
1 Peter 1:13 NCV

Young Amos Jacobs had given up on show business. But before quitting, he prayed a final prayer of desperation. The next day, he received a job offer that turned his career around. He changed his name to Danny Thomas, reinvigorated his showbiz career, and eventually became the beloved star of the popular TV sitcom *Make Room for Daddy*.

To give something back in gratitude for his blessings, Thomas endowed the St. Jude Children's Research Hospital in Memphis. He said, "Success has nothing to do with what you gain in life or accomplish for yourself. It's what you do for others."

If you desire to be a genuine success, make room to implement Danny's advice: find ways to give a little more than you get from life. If you do, your star, like Danny's, will keep shining today, tomorrow, and for generations to come.

You were created to add to life on earth,
not just take from it.
Rick Warren

Aim at Heaven

Set your minds on what is above,
not on what is on the earth.
Colossians 3:2 HCSB

If you wish to keep a comfortable conscience and a peaceful soul, you must distance yourself, at least somewhat, from the temptations and distractions around you. But distancing yourself isn't easy, especially when so many societal forces are struggling to get your attention, your participation, and your money.

C. S. Lewis advised, "Aim at heaven and you will get earth thrown in; aim at earth and you get neither." That's a wise reminder. You're likely to hit what you aim at, so aim high: aim at heaven. When you do, you'll be strengthening your character as you improve every aspect of your life. And God will demonstrate His approval as He showers you with more spiritual blessings than you can count.

Whoever seeks earth before he seeks heaven
will surely lose both earth and heaven.
St. John Chrysostom

Troubled Times

They won't be afraid of bad news; their hearts are steady because they trust the Lord.
Psalm 112:7 NCV

We live in a fearful world, a world where bad news travels at lightning speed and good news seems to move much slower. These are troubled times, times when we have legitimate concerns about the future of our nation, our world, and our families. But we also have every reason to live courageously. After all, since God has promised to love us and protect us, whom—or what—should we fear?

Perhaps you, like countless others, have found your courage tested by the anxieties and fears that are part of twenty-first-century life. If so, God left an important message for you sprinkled throughout the Bible: He wants you to think less about your challenges and more about His love. Remember that your heavenly Father is not just near; He is right here and He's ready to help. So let your faith in a faithful God bring you comfort today. When you trust Him, your heart can be steady even in troubled times.

When we submit difficult and alarming situations to God, He promises that His peace will be like a military garrison to guard our hearts from fear.
Dennis Swanberg

A Healing Touch

I am the Lord that healeth thee.

Exodus 15:26 KJV

Are you concerned about your spiritual, physical, or emotional health? If so, a timeless source of comfort and assurance is as near as your bookshelf. That source is the Bible.

God's Word has much to say about every aspect of life, including our health. When we face concerns of any sort–including health-related challenges–God is with us. So let your medical doctor do his or her part, but place your ultimate trust in the only One who can heal you.

Talk to God about your health, seek His guidance, and ask Him for the things you need. When you do, He will hear your prayers–and that's a comforting thing, because His healing touch, like His love, endures forever.

God helps the sick in two ways,
through the science of medicine and through
the science of faith and prayer.

Norman Vincent Peale

God's Gift of Family

You must choose for yourselves today whom you will serve. . . . As for me and my family, we will serve the Lord.

Joshua 24:15 NCV

In the life of every family, there are moments of frustration and disappointment—lots of them. But for those who are fortunate enough to live in the presence of a close-knit, caring clan, the rewards far outweigh the frustrations.

No family is perfect, including yours. But despite the inevitable challenges and hurt feelings of family life, your clan is God's gift to you. That little band of men, women, kids, and babies is a priceless treasure on temporary loan from the heavenly Father. Give thanks today for the gift of family. Enjoy the comfort of each other's presence. And determine that you and your family will serve the Lord.

Having family responsibilities and concerns just has to make you a more understanding person.

Sandra Day O'Connor

A Terrific Tomorrow

"I know what I am planning for you," says the Lord.
"I have good plans for you, not plans to hurt you.
I will give you hope and a good future."
Jeremiah 29:11 NCV

How bright does your future look? God has plans for your future that are so bright you'd be wise to bring several pairs of sunglasses and a lifetime supply of sunblock!

Still, the way you think about your future will play an important role in how your future unfolds. The phenomenon is called the "self-fulfilling prophecy"—what you predict will happen leads you to act in a certain way that causes that thing to happen.

Are you expecting a terrific tomorrow, or are you dreading a terrible one? The way you answer that question will also influence the way you act, and those actions can have a powerful impact on the way tomorrow unfolds.

Today, as you look to the future and make choices about how to live in the present, remember that God has an amazing plan for you. Act—and believe—accordingly. And don't forget the sunblock.

The future is as bright as the promises of God.
Adoniram Judson

Genuine Gratitude

I will give thanks to the Lord with all my heart;
I will tell of all Your wonders. I will be glad and exult
in You; I will sing praise to Your name, O Most High.

Psalm 9:1–2 NASB

We honor God, in part, by the genuine gratitude we feel in our hearts for the blessings He has bestowed upon us. Yet even the most saintly among us experiences periods of apathy, times when we are not fully aware of or fully grateful for the blessings and opportunities God has entrusted to our care. Why? Because we're imperfect human beings who are incapable of perfect gratitude.

Even on life's darker days, we must make the effort to cleanse our hearts of negative emotions and fill them, instead, with praise, with love, with hope, and with thanksgiving. When we do, we'll find an unexpected but undeniable comfort. We may not have perfect gratitude, but we can know and express genuine gratitude.

Contentment comes when we develop an attitude of gratitude for the important things we do have in our lives that we tend to take for granted if we have our eyes staring longingly at our neighbor's stuff.

Dave Ramsey

Transcendent Love

The Lord is good. His unfailing love continues forever, and his faithfulness continues to each generation.
Psalm 100:5 NLT

Where can we find God's love? Everywhere. God's love transcends space and time. It reaches beyond the heavens and it touches the darkest, smallest corner of every human heart. When we sincerely open our minds and hearts to God, we can experience His transcendent love at that moment and each moment for the rest of our lives.

God loves us in spite of our imperfections, in spite of our mistakes, our frailties, and our shortcomings. God loves us even when we don't love ourselves. His love never fails and never ends.

So today, take God at His word and accept Him with open arms. His transcendent love will surround you, comfort you, and transform you.

The great love of God is an ocean without a bottom or a shore.
C. H. Spurgeon

Love That Forgives

When you are praying, first forgive anyone you are holding a grudge against, so that your Father in heaven will forgive your sins, too.
Mark 11:25 NLT

Genuine love is an exercise in forgiveness. If we wish to build lasting relationships, we must learn to forgive. Why? Because our loved ones, like us, are imperfect.

Perhaps granting forgiveness is hard for you. If so, you're not alone. Genuine, lasting forgiveness can be difficult to achieve. Difficult but not impossible. With God's help, all things are possible, and that includes forgiveness.

God is willing to help you forgive others, but He also expects you to do some of the work. And make no mistake: forgiveness is work. It's not easy letting go of hurts or wrongs against us. God knows. He knows because He has suffered the wrongs and hurts we've inflicted on His heart. But we who know the comfort of His forgiveness should also be willing to share with others His gift of a love that forgives.

Forgiveness is the key to action and freedom.
Hannah Arendt

A Helping Hand

The greatest among you will be your servant.
For whoever exalts himself will be humbled,
and whoever humbles himself will be exalted.
Matthew 23:11–12 NIV

Jesus taught His followers about generosity. He taught that the most esteemed men and women should not be the self-congratulatory leaders of society, but rather the humblest of servants. If you were being graded on generosity, how would you score? Would you earn A's in philanthropy and humility? If your grades could stand a little improvement, this is the perfect day to begin.

Today you may feel the urge to hoard your blessings. Don't do it. Instead, give generously to your neighbors, and do so without fanfare. Find a need and fill it . . . humbly. Lend a helping hand or share a word of kindness. Vow to do whatever it takes to improve your little corner of the world.

The world says that the more you take,
the more you have. Christ says, the more you give, the more you are.
Frederick Buechner

Sparkle!

May the God of hope fill you with all joy and peace as you trust in him, so that you may overflow with hope by the power of the Holy Spirit.

Romans 15:13 NIV

Born in 1928, Shirley Temple became the biggest box-office draw in the United States by the tender age of ten. Amazingly, millions of fans still love to watch her childhood performances. What's the attraction for movies made so long ago? In many ways, the films seem as fresh today as they did then, in part because of the advice the young actress received from her mother.

Shirley's mother had a strategy that helped her daughter succeed. Just before the director shouted, "Action," Shirley's mom whispered one word in her daughter's ear: "Sparkle!" It was little Shirley's reminder to concentrate and give the performance her full attention.

All of us can benefit from the one-word cue that helped make Shirley Temple a star. So today, whether you're at work, home, school, or play, sparkle! Your audience will love you for it.

No person who is enthusiastic about his work has anything to fear from life.

Sam Goldwyn

Using Your Talents

"Master," he said, "you entrusted me with five talents. See, I have gained five more." His master replied, "Well done, good and faithful servant! You have been faithful with a few things; I will put you in charge of many things. Come and share your master's happiness!"

Matthew 25:20–21 NIV

Our talents, resources, and opportunities are all gifts from the Giver of all things good. And the best way to say thank you for these gifts is to use them.

Do you have a particular talent? Hone that skill and use it. Do you possess financial resources? Share them. Have you been blessed by a particular opportunity or unusual good fortune? Use your position to help others.

When you share the gifts God has given you—freely and without fanfare—you invite God to bless you more and more. So today, do yourself and the world a favor: be a faithful steward of the talents and treasures God has entrusted to you. Then prepare yourself for even greater blessings that are sure to come.

Employ whatever God has entrusted you with, in doing good, all possible good, in every possible kind and degree.

John Wesley

Carried in His Hand

I will be your God throughout your lifetime—until your hair is white with age. I made you, and I will care for you. I will carry you along and save you.

Isaiah 46:4 NLT

God has promised to lift you up and guide your steps if you'll follow Him. God has promised that when you entrust your life to Him completely and without reservation, He will give you the strength to meet any challenge, the courage to face any trial, and the wisdom to live in His righteousness.

God's hand uplifts those who turn their hearts and prayers to Him. Will you count yourself among that number? Will you accept God's comfort and wear God's armor against the temptations and distractions of our troubled world? If you do, you can live courageously and optimistically, knowing that you are carried by the comforting, loving, unfailing hand of God.

The God who spoke still speaks. He comes into our world. He comes into your world. He comes to do what you can't.

Max Lucado

Caring for Your Family

Each one of us needs to look after the good of the people around us, asking ourselves, "How can I help?"
Romans 15:2 MSG

At times, family life can be challenging—and demanding. Sometimes we wish we could withdraw from our responsibilities. But God has blessed us with families and He expects us to care for them.

As you think about your family today, ask yourself this question: "How can I help?" Consider who in your clan—including both your immediate and extended families—needs a kind word, a heartfelt hug, a phone call, a letter, or even an encouraging e-mail. Once you've decided who needs your help, take action today to show care for that loved one.

No family is perfect, but your clan is God's gift to you. They're a gift to be treasured. Today, give thanks for the many ways you enjoy the care and comfort of a family . . . and then offer that gift of care and comfort to them.

The miraculous thing about being a family is that in the last analysis, we are each dependent of one another and God, woven together by mercy given and mercy received.
Barbara Johnson

The Rewards of Courage

Don't be afraid, because I am your God.
I will make you strong and will help you;
I will support you with my right hand that saves you.
Isaiah 41:10 NCV

Eleanor Roosevelt, niece of President Theodore Roosevelt and wife of President Franklin D. Roosevelt, accomplished much as America's longest-tenured First Lady. This remarkable woman offered first-class advice when she said, "You gain strength, courage, and confidence every time you look fear in the face."

If you're looking for a way to get more out of your life, consider any irrational fears that may be holding you back. Face up to your fear of failure (we all experience it) and refuse to back down in the face of adversity. And, most important, entrust your way to the God who has promised to strengthen and help you. When you do these things, you'll see that courage is its own reward . . . but not its only reward.

Nothing in life is to be feared.
It is only to be understood.
Marie Curie

A Time to Grieve, a Time to Heal

They cried out to the Lord in their trouble, and He saved them out of their distresses.
Psalm 107:13 NKJV

The book of Ecclesiastes reminds us that there is a time for everything—a time for grief and a time for healing (3:3–4). Even if you're currently gripped by an overwhelming sense of disappointment or loss, rest assured that better days are ahead. The Bible tells us that if we cry out to God, He will help and save us.

Is your relationship with the Creator such that you call out to Him when you're grieving? If not, are you willing to establish a personal, intimate relationship with Him? Are you willing to trust Him and depend on Him? If so, you'll come to know the indescribable comfort that grief, however devastating, is temporary, but that God's love is forever.

God stands ready to offer His healing hand. He's waiting for you to reach out to Him. So why not take His hand today?

In the soul-searching of our lives,
we are to stay quiet so we can hear Him say
all that He wants to say to us in our hearts.
Charles Swindoll

Choosing to Forgive

Be kind to each other, tenderhearted, forgiving one another, just as God through Christ has forgiven you.
Ephesians 4:32 NLT

Finding comfort is so very difficult—perhaps impossible—until we summon the wisdom and courage to forgive those who have hurt us. Forgiveness is a choice. We decide whether to forgive those who have brought us harm in some way.

When we obey God by offering forgiveness to His children, we will be blessed and will receive His comfort. But when we allow bitterness and resentment to poison our hearts, we are victimized by our own shortsightedness.

Do you harbor resentment against anyone? If so, today you're faced with an important decision—whether to forgive the person who has hurt you or withhold that forgiveness and forfeit the comfort it can bring. Don't let another day slip away without choosing to forgive.

Forgiveness is God's command.
Martin Luther

A Day to Rejoice

Rejoice in the Lord, you righteous ones;
praise from the upright is beautiful.
Psalm 33:1 HCSB

This day is a blessed gift from God, and we have countless reasons to rejoice in it. Yet on some days, when the demands of life threaten to overwhelm us, we don't feel much like rejoicing. Instead of celebrating God's glorious creation, we may find ourselves wallowing in frustration and worried by uncertainties.

The familiar words of Psalm 118:24 remind us: "This is the day the Lord has made; let us rejoice and be glad in it" (NIV). Whatever this day holds for you, begin it and end it with God as your partner. Throughout the day, give thanks to the One who created you and saved you. God's love for you is infinite. What better reason to rejoice?

Write it on your heart that every day
is the best day of the year.
Ralph Waldo Emerson

Good Work

There is nothing better for people than to be happy in their work. That is why we are here!
Ecclesiastes 3:22 NLT

She acted in B movies and was cast in an old-time radio program, so she was certainly no major star. But all that changed when Lucille Ball, accompanied by her bandleader husband Desi Arnez, ventured into the then unproven medium of television. When their show captured the hearts of fans everywhere, Lucy became an icon.

Fans the world over still enjoy reruns of *I Love Lucy*. The show was, and is, fun to watch partly because it was fun to make. Lucy recalled, "We had more fun on the set than we ever had at any party after the show."

Doing good work can and should be a pleasure. So today, imitate America's favorite redhead by weaving a little merriment into your tasks. When you do good work and have fun doing it, your star is sure to shine.

To love what you do and feel that it matters–how could anything be more fun?
Katherine Graham

July 21

Waiting Quietly for God

I wait for the Lord; I wait, and put my hope in His word.
Psalm 130:5 HCSB

The Bible instructs us to wait quietly for the Lord, but as busy folks with too many obligations and too few hours in which to fulfill them, we find that waiting quietly for God can be difficult indeed. We know what we want and when we want it—sooner rather than later. But God operates according to His own perfect timetable and if we're wise, we will trust His plans—even when they differ from our own.

We would do well to be patient in all things. We must be patient with our families, our friends, and our associates. But we must also be patient with our Creator as He works out His plan for our lives. And that's as it should be. After all, think how patient God has been with us.

The key to everything is patience.
You get the chicken by hatching the egg,
not be smashing it.
Ellen Glasgow

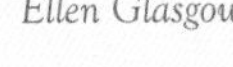

Contentment That Lasts

Serving God does make us very rich, if we are satisfied with what we have. We brought nothing into the world, so we can take nothing out. But, if we have food and clothes, we will be satisfied with that.

1 Timothy 6:6–8 NCV

The preoccupation with happiness and contentment is ubiquitous in our modern world. We're bombarded with messages that claim to tell us where to find peace and comfort in a world that worships materialism and wealth. But lasting contentment is not found in material possessions; true contentment is a spiritual gift from God to those who trust in Him and follow His path.

Would you like to be a more contented person? Would you like to experience the kind of comfort and joy that money can never buy? Then don't depend on the world to make you happy, and don't expect material possessions to bring you real contentment. Contentment that lasts begins with God, so turn your thoughts and prayers to Him. You'll find you can be more than satisfied with that.

The heart is rich when it is content, and it is always content when its desires are set upon God.

Saint Miguel of Ecuador

Do Something

Observe people who are good at their work—skilled workers are always in demand and admired.

Proverbs 22:29 MSG

Walter Cronkite quit school after his junior year at the University of Texas and began a series of newspaper reporting jobs. Thus began one of the most memorable journalistic careers in modern history. Cronkite was a war correspondent during World War II, and in time he became a fixture in American homes as the news anchor at CBS. A 1973 opinion poll even voted him the most trusted man in America.

Cronkite once observed, "I never had the ambition to be something. I had the ambition to do something." If you want to be someone special, don't aspire to public acclaim; aspire to excellence. Then, like Walter Cronkite, you'll discover that your audience is more likely to notice your work when you let that work speak for itself.

Excellence is not an act but a habit.
The things you do the most are the things
you will do best.

Marva Collins

Comforting Friends

As iron sharpens iron, so a friend sharpens a friend.
Proverbs 27:17 NLT

Where can we turn for comfort? One place we can turn is to our friends. Loyal friends have much to offer us—encouragement, faith, fellowship, fun, and comfort, for starters. Throughout the Bible, God reminds us to love one another, to care for one another, and to treat one another as we wish to be treated. When we live by God's Golden Rule, we help build His kingdom here on earth.

Today, resolve to be a trustworthy, encouraging, loyal friend. And treasure the people in your life who are loyal friends to you. Friendship is a glorious gift, provided and blessed by God. Give thanks for that gift and nurture it.

Friendship plays an important role in God's plan for His world and for your life. He blesses you through your friends and if you let Him, He'll use you to bless your friends as well.

I hope you will find a few folks who walk with God to also walk with you through the seasons of your life.
John Eldredge

A Clear Conscience

Let us come near to God with a sincere heart and a sure faith, because we have been made free from a guilty conscience, and our bodies have been washed with pure water.

Hebrews 10:22 NCV

Few things in life provide more comfort than a clear conscience. In fact, a clear conscience is one of the undeniable blessings we receive whenever we allow God to guide our path through the trials and temptations of everyday life.

Have you formed the habit of listening carefully to that still, small voice of God's Spirit? If you're wise, you'll listen to what it has to say and behave accordingly. That little voice has much to teach us about the decisions we make and the way we choose to live.

Today, as you make the myriad decisions about what you do and say, let the Spirit's voice be your guide. When you do, you'll enjoy the refreshing feeling of having a clear conscience before God.

To go against one's conscience is neither safe nor right. Here I stand; I cannot do otherwise.

Martin Luther

Your Mission

Be strong and courageous, and do the work.
Do not be afraid or discouraged, for the Lord God,
my God, is with you.
1 Chronicles 28:20 NIV

Fred Rogers was an ordained minister who wrote more than two hundred songs, but he will forever be remembered as the beloved friend and mentor to millions of children—the soft-spoken television icon who created *Mister Rogers' Neighborhood.*

Rogers observed, "Each of us has only one life on this earth, and we should use it." As usual, Mr. Rogers was right.

Fred Rogers followed his own advice, and so should you. God created you for a purpose, and He'll do His part to help you find and fulfill it. In turn, He asks you to make your life a mission, not an intermission. So get busy. You have important work to do in your neighborhood.

Whatever purpose motivates your life,
it must be something big enough and grand enough to
make the investment worthwhile.
Warren Wiersbe

Enthusiastic Discipleship

Do your work with enthusiasm.
Work as if you were serving the Lord, not as if you were serving only men and women.
Ephesians 6:7 NCV

With whom will you choose to walk today? Will you walk with shortsighted people who honor the ways of the world, or will you walk with the Son of God? Jesus wants to walk with you. Will you choose to walk with Him today and every day of your life?

Jesus has called on people of every generation (and that includes you) to follow in His footsteps. And He promised that when we do, our burdens will be light (Matthew 11:28–30).

Jesus doesn't want you to be a run-of-the-mill, follow-the-crowd kind of person. He wants you to be a "new creation" through Him. And that's the best thing you could want for yourself. Today, undertake each task enthusiastically, remembering that you do it not just for others but for God. Then you'll know the joy of discipleship.

Being a disciple involves becoming a learner,
a student of the Master.
Charles Stanley

Heeding God's Call

You did not choose me, but I chose you and appointed you to go and bear fruit—fruit that will last.

John 15:16 NIV

God is calling you to follow a specific path that He has chosen for your life. And it is vitally important that you heed that call. Otherwise, your talents may not reach their full potential, and precious opportunities may be lost forever.

Have you already heard God's call? Are you pursuing it with vigor? If so, you're both blessed and wise. But if you have not yet discovered what God intends for you to do with your life, keep searching and praying until you discover why the Creator put you here.

Remember that God has important work for you to do—work designed specifically for you. He has placed you in a particular location, amid selected people, with unique opportunities to serve. And He will give you all the tools you need to succeed. So listen for His voice, watch for His leading, and step out in faith to heed His call.

The place where God calls you is the place where your deep gladness and the world's deep hunger meet.

Frederick Buechner

To God Be the Glory

God is against the proud, but he gives grace to the humble.
1 Peter 5:5 NCV

Would you like to enjoy a more peaceful, grace-filled life? Then spend more time meditating on God's greatness than on your own. Contemplate your blessings and be sure to give credit where credit is due—to your Creator.

Dietrich Bonhoeffer said, "It is very easy to overestimate the importance of our own achievements in comparison with what we owe others." We are imperfect human beings who sometimes like to inflate our accomplishments.

But reality breeds humility. When we see ourselves in light of God's glory, we realize that he alone is worthy of praise. Instead of puffing out our chests and saying, "Look at us!" we should give glory to God. When we do, we'll know the incomparable comfort of His grace poured out on our hearts and lives.

What makes humility so desirable is the marvelous thing it does to us; it creates in us a capacity for the closest possible intimacy with God.
Monica Baldwin

A Dose of Laughter

A happy heart is like good medicine.
Proverbs 17:22 NCV

Laughter is medicine for the soul, but sometimes, amid the stresses of the day, we forget to take our medicine. Instead of viewing our world with a mixture of optimism and humor, we allow worries and distractions to rob us of the joy God intends for our lives.

So the next time you find yourself dwelling on the negatives of life, refocus your attention to things positive. The next time you fall prey to the blight of pessimism, turn your mind to happier thoughts.

When you think of your glass as half-empty, enjoy one of the few times it's comforting to be wrong. With God, your glass is never half-empty. With God as your companion and eternal hope, your glass is really full and overflowing. With Him, you can have a happy heart.

Mirth is God's medicine.
Everybody ought to bathe in it.
Henry Ward Beecher

Happy Day

How happy is everyone who fears the Lord,
who walks in His ways!
Psalm 128:1 HCSB

All too often, people think of happiness as a condition known in the past or as something they may experience someday in the distant future—but they're mistaken. Happiness, if it occurs at all, lives in the present tense; happiness can be found in each precious moment.

Are you willing to celebrate your life today? After all, this day—and each moment in it—is a blessed gift from God. When you stop to think about it, you probably have many reasons to rejoice.

So whatever this day holds for you, know that it can be a happy day when you trust God and follow Him. Throughout this day, give thanks to the One who created you. God's love for you is infinite. Accept it joyfully . . . and be happy.

[Men spend their lives in anticipation, in determining to be vastly happy at some period or other, when they have time.] The present time has one advantage over every other: it is our own.
Charles Caleb Colton

August

Following God's Instructions

The world and its desires pass away, but the man who does the will of God lives forever.
1 John 2:17 NIV

God has given us a priceless guidebook for life. It's called the Bible and it contains comprehensive instructions which, if followed, lead to fulfillment and comfort in this life–as well as eternal life in heaven. At times we're all tempted to disregard the instructions in God's Word–after all, we are only human. But the better way is to study God's Word seriously and follow His instructions carefully.

Talking about God is easy; living by His guidelines is considerably more difficult, but it's also more rewarding. When we obey the Father, He showers us with enough spiritual blessings for the day ahead *and* for all eternity.

So what's the best way to proclaim our love for the Creator? By obeying Him. And for further instructions, read the Manual.

Happiness is obedience, and obedience is happiness.
C. H. Spurgeon

Good Pressures, Bad Pressures

My dear friend, do not follow what is bad;
follow what is good.
3 John 11 NCV

Our world is filled with pressures–some good, some bad. The pressures we feel to follow God's will and obey His commandments are positive pressures. God places them on our hearts, and He intends that we act in accordance with His leading. But we also face different pressures, ones that lead us away from God's path for our lives. And of those we must beware.

Sometimes society applies strong negative pressures upon us. That's when we can turn to caring friends and to family members for support . . . and we can turn to God.

God seeks to mold us into new beings who are not conformed to this world. By following God's path–and by resisting society's negative influences–we please the Creator . . . and we will be blessed.

I have found that the closer I am to the godly people
around me, the easier it is for me to live
a righteous life because they hold me accountable.
John MacArthur

When the Answer Is No

He looks to the ends of the earth
and sees everything under the heavens.
Job 28:24 HCSB

God does not always answer our prayers as soon as we might like, and He doesn't always answer our prayers by saying yes. God isn't an order taker, and He's not some sort of cosmic vending machine dispensing goodies at our every request.

Sometimes—even when we want something desperately—our loving, heavenly Father responds by saying no. Although it's difficult, we must remember that if we accept His answer, even if we don't understand it, it will be for our good in the end.

God answers prayers not only according to our wishes, but also according to His master plan. We cannot know that plan, but we can know the Planner . . . and we can trust His wisdom, His righteousness, His mercy, and His love. God sees everything, including what's truly best for us.

Let's never forget that some of God's greatest mercies are His refusals. He says no in order that He may, in some way we cannot imagine, say yes. All His ways with us are merciful. His meaning is always love.

Elisabeth Elliot

Taking Risks

Is anything too hard for the Lord?
Genesis 18:14 NKJV

As we consider the uncertainties of the future, we're often confronted with a powerful temptation: the temptation to "play it safe." Unwilling to move mountains, we fret over molehills. Unwilling to entertain great hopes for tomorrow, we focus on the unfairness of today. Unwilling to trust God completely, we take timid half steps when God wants us to take giant leaps.

Today, ask God for the courage to step beyond the boundaries of your doubts. Ask Him to guide you to a place where you can realize your full potential–a place where you are freed from the fear of failure. Ask Him to do His part, and promise Him that you will do your part. Don't ask Him to lead you to a "safe" place; ask Him to lead you to the "right" place . . . and remember that those two places are seldom the same.

Avoiding danger is no safer in the long run
than outright exposure.
The fearful are caught as often as the bold.
Helen Keller

Finding Comfort and Peace

The peace of God, which surpasses all comprehension, will guard your hearts and your minds in Christ Jesus.
Philippians 4:7 NASB

We are imperfect human beings who possess imperfect faith. So it's not surprising that we lose hope from time to time. When we do, we need the encouragement of friends and the life-changing power of prayer.

If we find ourselves falling into the spiritual traps of discouragement or despair, we can seek guidance from God and solicit support from our family members and friends.

Peace, joy, and contentment are gifts from God, and they're available to all who will take the steps necessary to claim them. When we guard ourselves against the spiritual snares that seek to entrap us—things like worry, discouragement, or fear—and choose instead to trust God, He will grant us the peace, the contentment, and the power that can and should be ours.

Peace and love are always alive in us,
but we are not always alive to peace and love.
Juliana of Norwich

Strength for the Struggle

O Lord, you are my lamp.
The Lord lights up my darkness.
2 Samuel 22:29 NLT

Life is a tapestry of good days and bad days, but for most of us, the good days predominate. For that very reason, sometimes it's easy to take our blessings for granted (a temptation we must resist with all our might). But during life's difficult days, we discover precisely what we're made of. And, more important, we discover what our faith is made of.

Has your faith been put to the test? If so, you know that with God's help, you can endure life's darker days. Remembering that is important, because when your faith is again put to the test—as it likely will be—you can rest assured that God is perfectly willing, and always ready, to give you strength for the struggle.

The ultimate measure of a man is not where
he stands in moments of comfort and convenience,
but where he stands at times of challenge
and controversy.
Martin Luther King Jr.

The Courage to Live Boldly

God doesn't want us to be shy with his gifts,
but bold and loving and sensible.
2 Timothy 1:7 MSG

Do you prefer to face your fears rather than run from them? If so, you will be blessed because of your willingness to live courageously.

When the apostle Paul wrote to Timothy, he reminded his young protégé that the God they served was a bold God and that God's Spirit empowered His children with boldness. Like Timothy, we face times of uncertainty and fear. God's message is the same to us today as it was to Timothy: we can live boldly—and we should.

So today, as you face the challenges that come your way, remember that God is with you. With His help and comfort, you can find the courage to live boldly.

We must have courage to be happy.
Henri Frédéric Amiel

Hope and Happiness

I will always have hope;
I will praise you more and more.
Psalm 71:14 NIV

Hope and happiness are traveling companions. After all, God is good and His love endures; we have every reason to be hopeful. But sometimes, in life's darker moments, it's easy to lose sight of these blessings, and when we do, it's easy to lose hope. Yet if we sincerely desire to lead happier, healthier lives, we will learn to live by faith.

Are you a hope-filled person? You should be. You have an array of talents within you and an assortment of opportunities before you. You have the potential to achieve your goals and the wherewithal to realize your dreams. So today, praise God for His goodness toward you and walk confidently toward your horizon with assurance and hope, knowing that your loving, heavenly Father walks with you every step of the way.

All things are possible for him who believes,
more to him who hopes,
even more to him who loves.
St. Lawrence of Brindisi

Caring for the Downtrodden

Whatever you did for one of the least of these brothers of mine, you did for me.

Matthew 25:40 NIV

How fortunate we are to live in a land of opportunities and possibilities. But for many people around the world, the kind of opportunities we enjoy are scarce. In too many parts of the globe, hardworking men and women struggle merely to provide food and shelter for their families.

Because much has been given to us, much is expected. Because so many material blessings have been entrusted to our care, we should be quick to share our possessions with others, wherever they are.

When we care for the downtrodden, when we show compassion for those who suffer, we follow the instructions of the One who created us. What sweet comfort and joy to know that what we do for others, we do for God.

How wonderful it is that nobody need wait
a single moment before starting
to improve the world.

Anne Frank

His Awesome Creation

God saw all that He had made, and behold,
it was very good.
Genesis 1:31 NASB

When we consider God's glorious universe, we marvel at the miracle of nature. The smallest seedlings and grandest stars are all part of God's creation. He has placed His handiwork on display for all to see, and if we'll make time each day to celebrate the world that surrounds us, it can do wonders for our well-being.

Today, even as you busy yourself with the demands of life, pause to consider the majesty of heaven and earth. God's creation is as miraculous as it is beautiful, as incomprehensible as it is breathtaking.

The psalmist reminds us that the heavens are a declaration of God's glory (Psalm 19:1). May we never cease to praise the Father for a universe that stands as an awesome testimony to His presence and His power.

No philosophical theory which I have
yet come across is a radical improvement
on the words of Genesis, that
"in the beginning God made Heaven and Earth."
C. S. Lewis

God's Surprising Plans for You

I will guide you along the best pathway for your life.
I will advise you and watch over you.
Psalm 32:8 NLT

God's Word indicates that when we do our duties in small matters, He will give us additional responsibilities (Matthew 25:14–21). Sometimes those responsibilities come when God changes the course of our lives so that we may better serve Him. Sometimes our rewards come in the form of temporary setbacks that lead, in turn, to greater victories. Sometimes God rewards us by saying no to our requests so that He can say yes to a far grander gift that we, in our limited understanding, would never have thought to ask for.

If you seek to be God's servant in great matters, be faithful, be patient, and be dutiful in smaller matters. Then step back and watch as God surprises you with the spectacular creativity of His infinite wisdom and His perfect plan.

Every man's life is a plan of God.
Horace Bushnell

Strength for the Day

The Lord is a refuge for His people and a stronghold.
Joel 3:16 NASB

Have you made God the cornerstone of your life, or is He relegated to a few hours on Sunday morning? Have you genuinely allowed God to reign over every corner of your heart, or have you attempted to place Him in a limited "spiritual compartment"? How you answer these questions reveals some truth about your relationship with your heavenly Father. When you trust God with your life, you'll find that He's a refuge and a source of strength you can turn to throughout your day and throughout your life.

God loves you. In times of trouble, He will comfort you; in times of sorrow, He will dry your tears. When you are weak or sorrowful, remember that God is as near as your next breath. He stands at the door of your heart, waiting and longing for your invitation. Welcome Him in and trust Him to guide you. Today, accept the peace, the strength, and the comfort that only God can give.

In my weakness, I have learned, like Moses, to lean hard on God. The weaker I am, the harder I lean on Him. The harder I lean, the stronger I discover Him to be. The stronger I discover God to be, the more resolute I am in this job He's given me to do.

Joni Eareckson Tada

Simple Wisdom

Don't abandon wisdom, and she will watch over you; love her, and she will guard you.

Proverbs 4:6 HCSB

Robert Fulghum's most popular book was titled *All I Really Need to Know I Learned in Kindergarten.* As the title makes clear, Fulghum's philosophy isn't comprised of complex philosophies or obtuse truisms. He observed, "What's necessary to live a meaningful life—that isn't all that complicated. . . . Wisdom was not at the top of the graduate-school mountain, but there in the sandpile at Sunday School."

If you're looking for a surefire way to improve your life, try the advice Fulghum offers in his book. Follow the rules you learned as a kid: be polite, tell the truth, clean up your messes, play fair, and do the right thing. You'll discover that being a responsible grown-up is not as complicated as it seems. In fact, sometimes it's as simple as child's play.

Things should be made as simple as possible.

Albert Einstein

When We Grieve

God will wipe away every tear from their eyes.
Revelation 7:17 HCSB

Grief visits all of us who live long and love deeply. When we lose a loved one, or when we experience any other profound loss, darkness can overwhelm us for a while, and we feel we cannot summon the strength to face another day. But with God's help, we can.

God assures us that He is "close to the brokenhearted" (Psalm 34:18 NIV). In times of intense sadness, we can turn to Him. When we do, He will comfort us . . . and in time, our tears will be wiped away.

Concentration-camp survivor Corrie ten Boom once said, "There is no pit so deep that God's love is not deeper still." Let us remember those words and live by them . . . especially when we grieve.

God whispers to us in our pleasures,
speaks to us in our conscience,
but shouts in our pains.
C. S. Lewis

Moving Beyond Worry

Blessed is he who trusts in the Lord.
Proverbs 16:20 NIV

Because life is sometimes difficult, and because we (understandably) feel fear and uncertainty about the future, we worry. At times we may find ourselves fretting over countless details of life. We fret about our relationships, our finances, our health, or any number of potential problems, some large and some small.

If you're a worrier by nature, perhaps it's time to rethink the way you think. Have you formed the unhelpful habit of focusing too intently on negative aspects of life while spending too little time counting your blessings? If so, take your worries to God today and leave them with Him. When you do, you'll learn to worry a little less and to trust God a little more—and that's as it should be, because God is trustworthy . . . and He's looking out for you.

If you can't sleep, don't count sheep;
talk to the Shepherd.
Source unknown

Love Is a Choice

Beloved, if God so loved us,
we also ought to love one another.
1 John 4:11 NASB

Love begins and ends with God, but the middle part belongs to us. During the brief time that we have here on earth, God has given each of us the opportunity to become a loving person, to be kind, to be courteous, to be cooperative, and to be forgiving—to obey the Golden Rule. Unfortunately, sometimes we try to make up our own rules as we go.

If we choose to reject the many opportunities God has given us to show love to others, we cheat ourselves out of His incomparable rewards.

The decisions we make, and the results of those decisions, affect the quality of our relationships. God has taken the first step: He loved us even before we loved Him. Today, choose to show love not only to your heavenly Father, but also to those He has placed in your path.

How do you spell love? When you reach the point where the happiness, security, and development of another person is as much of a driving force to you as your own happiness, security, and development, then you have a mature love. True love is spelled G-I-V-E.

Josh McDowell

Beyond Materialism

What will it profit a man if he gains the whole world,
and loses his own soul?
Or what will a man give in exchange for his soul?
Mark 8:36–37 NKJV

In modern society, we need money to live. But if we're wise, we'll never make the acquisition of money the central focus of our lives. Money is a tool, but it should never overwhelm our sensibilities. Our focus should be on things spiritual, not things material. Yet the world encourages us to do the opposite.

The world glorifies material possessions, but God values our souls. Whenever we place our love for material possessions above our love for God, we make ourselves less comfortable, less contented, less satisfied with life. We do harm to our souls.

So today, free yourself from the chains of materialism. Nourish your soul by moving beyond the material to the spiritual. Peace and comfort are waiting for you there.

Keeping up with the Joneses is like keeping up
with a scared jackrabbit–only harder.
Marie T. Freeman

He Reigns

In all your ways acknowledge Him,
and He shall direct your paths.
Proverbs 3:6 NKJV

God is sovereign. He reigns over the entire universe, and He's directing your little corner of the world too. Your challenge is to recognize God's sovereignty and live in accordance with His directions. Of course, sometimes this is easier said than done.

Your heavenly Father may not always reveal His will as quickly (or as clearly) as you'd like. But rest assured: God is in control. He is right here with you and He wants to use you in wonderful, exciting ways.

Today, as you fulfill the responsibilities of everyday life, keep God in His rightful place—first place. When you do, He'll lead you along a path of His choosing. You need only watch, listen, learn . . . and follow.

Sovereignty means that God alone
ultimately has the right to declare
what creation should be.
Stanley Grenz

Seeking God's Will

Teach me to do Your will, for You are my God;
Your Spirit is good. Lead me in the land of uprightness.
Psalm 143:10 NKJV

God has a plan for our world and for our lives. The Creator does nothing by accident; He is willful and intentional. Unfortunately for us, we cannot always understand the will of the Father. Why? Because we are mortal beings with limited understanding. Although we cannot fully comprehend the will of God, we should always trust the will of God.

As this day unfolds, seek to know God's will and to obey His instructions. When you entrust your life to Him without reservation, He will give you wisdom, courage, and comfort. So don't wait another day—seek God's will today. Follow His lead. Trust His guidance, and accept His love. His Spirit is good, and His will is to lead you to a land of uprightness . . . and eternal blessing.

"If the Lord will" is not just a statement on a person's lips; it is the constant attitude of his heart.
Warren Wiersbe

A Helping Hand

The Samaritan . . . put the hurt man on his own donkey and took him to an inn where he cared for him.

Luke 10:33–34 NCV

Sometimes we'd like to help make the world a better place, but we're not sure how to do it. Jesus told the story of the good Samaritan, a man who helped a fellow traveler when no one else would. He told this story to show that we, too, should lend a hand when we encounter people who need our help.

When bad things happen in our world, there's always something we can do. What can you do today to make God's world a better place? You can start by making your own corner of the world a little happier by sharing kind words and good deeds. And when you become aware of people's needs—and you've done what you can to meet those needs—take those concerns to God in prayer. Whether you've offered a helping hand or a heartfelt prayer, you've done a lot.

Make it a rule, and pray to God to help you to keep it, never, if possible, to lie down at night without being able to say: "I have made one human being at least a little wiser, or a little happier, or at least a little better this day."

Charles Kingsley

Look Before You Leap

An impulsive vow is a trap;
later you'll wish you could get out of it.
Proverbs 20:25 MSG

Are you sometimes just a little too impulsive? Do you occasionally leap before you look? If so, you may find it helpful (and ultimately comforting) to take a careful look at what the Bible says about impulsiveness.

In Proverbs we are taught to be thoughtful, not reckless. Yet the world often tempts us to behave recklessly. Sometimes we're faced with powerful temptations to be impulsive, undisciplined. These are temptations we must resist.

When you make a habit of thinking first and acting second, you'll be comforted in the knowledge that you're incorporating God's wisdom into the fabric of your life. And you'll reap the rewards the Creator bestows on wise folks (like you) who take the time to look–and think–before they leap.

Delay is preferable to error.
Thomas Jefferson

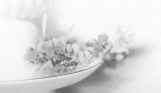

Your Spiritual Health

I love you, O Lord, my strength.
Psalm 18:1 NIV

C. S. Lewis said, "A man's spiritual health is exactly proportional to his love for God." So if we are to enjoy the spiritual health God intends for us, we need to develop the proper love for God. We do that partly when we worship Him and obey Him.

When we worship God faithfully and obediently, we invite His love into our hearts. When we truly worship God, by allowing Him to rule over our days and our lives, we'll sense His presence and His love for us. That, in turn, leads us to grow to love God even more deeply.

Today, open your heart to the Father. When you do, your spiritual health will improve . . . and so will every other aspect of your life.

He who is filled with love is filled with God Himself.
St. Augustine

Your Spiritual Journey

Leave inexperience behind, and you will live;
pursue the way of understanding.
Proverbs 9:6 HCSB

Gaining spiritual maturity takes time. Few among us possess the insight or the discipline to become "instant saints." And that's perfectly okay with God. He understands that none of us is perfect and that we all have room for personal, emotional, and spiritual growth.

Life is a series of decisions. Each day we make countless choices that can bring us closer to God . . . or pull us away from Him. When we live according to the principles contained in God's Word, we embark on a journey toward spiritual maturity that results in life abundant and life eternal.

Are you feeling less than perfect today? If so, don't fret. You don't have to be perfect to be wonderful. And even though you'll never achieve complete spiritual maturity in this lifetime, you can still keep growing—today and every day. When you do, the results will be wonderful.

You've got to continue to grow, or you're just like last night's cornbread: stale and dry.
Loretta Lynn

Making Peace with Your Past

Forget about what's happened; don't keep going over old history. Be alert, be present. I'm about to do something brand-new. It's bursting out! Don't you see it? There it is! I'm making a road through the desert, rivers in the badlands.

Isaiah 43:18–19 MSG

Because we're human, we can be slow to forget yesterday's disappointments. But if we sincerely seek to focus our hopes and energies on the future, then we must find ways to accept the past, no matter how difficult it may be to do so.

Have you made peace with your past? If so, congratulations. But if you're mired in the quicksand of remorse or regret, it's time to escape the morass. How can you do so? By accepting what has been and by trusting God for what will be.

If you have not yet made peace with the past, today is the day to declare an end to all hostilities. Then you can turn your thoughts to the wondrous promises of God and to the glorious future He has in store for you.

The life you have led doesn't need to be the only life you'll have.

Anna Quindlen

Pause for Praise

Praise the Lord. Give thanks to the Lord, for he is good; his love endures forever.
Psalm 106:1 NIV

Sometimes, in our rush to get things done, we don't stop long enough to pause and thank our Creator for the countless blessings He has bestowed upon us. After all, we're busy people with many demands on our time; we have so much to do. But when we slow down long enough to express our gratitude to the One who made us, we enrich our own lives and the lives of those around us.

Thanksgiving should become a habit, a regular part of our daily routines. God has blessed us beyond measure and we owe Him everything, including our time and praise.

So today, pause and count your blessings. Then give thanks to the Giver of every good gift. God's love for you is never ending; your praise for Him should be never ending too.

Be not afraid of saying too much in the praises of God; all the danger is of saying too little.
Matthew Henry

Solving Problems

People who do what is right may have many problems,
but the Lord will solve them all.
Psalm 34:19 NCV

Life is an exercise in problem solving. The question is not whether we will encounter problems; the question is how we will choose to address them. When it comes to solving the problems of everyday living, we often know precisely what needs to be done, but we may be slow in doing it—especially if what needs to be done is difficult or uncomfortable for us. So we put off till tomorrow what should be done today.

The words of Psalm 34 remind us that the Lord solves problems for "people who do what is right." And usually, doing what's right means doing the uncomfortable work of confronting our problems sooner rather than later. What problems do you have today? Do what's right, and take them to the Lord. He'll help you solve them.

If you simply let a problem wash around in your mind, it will seem greater and much more vague than it will appear on close examination.

Dorothea Brande

Being Still

Be still, and know that I am God.
Psalm 46:10 NKJV

The world seems to grow louder day by day, and we can feel as though our senses are assaulted at every turn. If we allow the distractions of a clamorous society to separate us from God's peace, we do ourselves a profound disservice. As thoughtful adults, we must carve out moments of silence in a world filled with noise. If we'll quiet our minds and our hearts, we'll learn that we can sense God's will and His love.

Has the busy pace of life robbed you of the peace and comfort God has promised? If so, determine to be still and spend time communing with your Creator. Nothing is more important than the time you spend with your heavenly Father. Today, claim the inner peace that can be found in the silent moments you spend with God.

Most of man's trouble comes
from his inability to be still.
Blaise Pascal

August 28

Under Control

People may make plans in their minds,
but the Lord decides what they will do.
Proverbs 16:9 NCV

If you're like most people, you like being in control. You want things to happen according to your wishes and your timetable. But sometimes God has other plans and, ultimately, He will have the final word.

Are you embittered by a personal tragedy, something you didn't deserve and cannot understand? If so, it's time to make peace with life . . . and with God. It's time to forgive others and, if necessary, to forgive yourself. It's time to accept the unchangeable past, to embrace the priceless present, and to have faith in the promise of tomorrow. And it's time to trust God completely.

If you've encountered unfortunate circumstances that are beyond your control, trust God who *is* in control. When you place your faith in Him, you can be comforted in the knowledge that He is both loving and wise, and that He understands His plans perfectly, even when you do not.

Acceptance is resting in God's goodness,
believing that He has all things under His control.
Charles Swindoll

The Rock

The Lord is my rock and my fortress and my deliverer;
the God of my strength, in whom I will trust.
2 Samuel 22:2–3 NKJV

Although blinded as an infant, Frances Crosby went on to become one of America's most beloved writers of religious poetry and hymns. She wrote more than nine thousand hymns; she spent her life teaching and serving the needy; and she was one of the most admired writers of the nineteenth century. Better known as Fanny Crosby, she was the woman who penned the classic hymn "Blessed Assurance."

Crosby was never embittered by her blindness. She saw her handicap as a stepping-stone, not a stumbling block.

Are you letting some "handicap" hold you back? Take a lesson from Fanny Crosby, and focus on your blessings, not your misfortunes. Build your life on the Rock that cannot be shaken—God. When you trust Him, you'll be able to overcome your own handicaps in life and enjoy the blessed assurance only God can give.

The size of your burden is never as important
as the way you carry it.
Lena Horne

Pushing Past Procrastination

If you make a promise to God, don't be slow to keep it. God is not happy with fools, so give God what you promised.
Ecclesiastes 5:4 NCV

If you've acquired the habit of putting off until tomorrow what needs to be done today, you know that procrastination can make you feel uncomfortable . . . sometimes very uncomfortable. So if you'd like to feel a little better about yourself and your world, try this: make it a habit to do things in the order of their importance, not in the order of your preference. When you do, you'll discover how good it feels to finish the difficult work first, rather than putting it off until the last possible minute.

Once you acquire the habit of doing first things first, you'll dramatically reduce your stress. You'll be more productive. You'll even sleep better at night.

So learn to defeat procrastination by pushing past your uneasiness and focusing on the big rewards you'll receive when you finish your work. It's the productive–and the peaceful–way to live.

Don't duck the most difficult problems. That just insures that the hardest part will be left when you're most tired. Get the big one done, and it's all downhill from then on.
Norman Vincent Peale

When the World Demands Perfection

A devout life does bring wealth,
but it's the rich simplicity of being yourself before God.
1 Timothy 6:6 MSG

Face it: sometimes it can be tough to respect yourself, especially if you're feeling like a less-than-perfect citizen living in a world that seems to demand perfection. But before you plunge headlong into self-critical thoughts, consider this: God knows all your imperfections, all your faults, and all your shortcomings . . . and He loves you anyway. And because God loves you, you can–and should–feel good about the person you see when you look in the mirror.

God's love is bigger and more powerful than anyone (even you) can imagine, but it's no fairy tale; His love is real. So do yourself a favor today: accept God's love with open arms. Whenever you have a moment when you don't love yourself very much, stop and remember this: God does loves you . . . a lot. And God is always right.

When everything has to be right, something isn't.
Stanislaw Lec

September

Feeling Good About Your Abilities

There are varieties of gifts, but the same Spirit.
And there are varieties of ministries, and the same Lord.
1 Corinthians 12:4–5 NASB

God has given each of us gifts. You have an array of talents, and no doubt some of those you've refined—and some still need to be refined. But nobody will force you to do the hard work of converting raw talent into prime-time talent. It's a job you must do for yourself. That may sound difficult, but the truth is, you'll feel better about yourself when you hone your abilities.

Today, make a promise to yourself and to your Creator that you will earnestly seek to discover and refine the talents He has given you. Ask Him to help you nourish those talents and make them grow. And then get down to the business of why you were blessed with such abilities to begin with; vow to share your gifts with the world for as long as God gives you the power to do so.

When I stand before God at the end of my life,
I would hope that I would not have a single bit
of talent left, and could say,
"I used everything You gave me."
Erma Bombeck

Simply Rich

A simple life in the Fear-of-God is better than a rich life with a ton of headaches.

Proverbs 15:16 MSG

Is yours a life of moderation or accumulation? Are you more interested in the possessions you can acquire or in the person you can become? The answers to these questions will go a long way in setting your direction for this day and, in time, the direction of your life.

In our affluent society, countless people and corporations vie for your attention, for your time, and for your dollars. Don't let them succeed in complicating your life! Keep your eyes–and your life–focused on God.

If your material possessions are somehow distancing you from your heavenly Father, discard them. If your outside interests leave you too little time for your family or your faith, slow down the merry-go-round–or better yet, get off the merry-go-round completely. Is your life full of headaches? Get back to the simple yet abundant life only God can offer, and you'll find those headaches melting away.

A man is rich in proportion to the number of things he can afford to let alone.

Henry David Thoreau

Rejoicing Hearts

Let the hearts of those who seek the Lord rejoice.
Look to the Lord and his strength; seek his face always.
1 Chronicles 16:10–11 NIV

What is your attitude today? Are you fearful or worried? Are you more concerned about pleasing your friends than about pleasing your God? Are you bitter, confused, cynical, or pessimistic? If so, it's time to have a little chat with your Father in heaven.

God wants to fill your life with spiritual abundance and joy—but He won't force His joy upon you—you must claim it for yourself. So today, do yourself this favor: accept God's gifts with a smile on your face, a song on your lips, and joy in your heart.

Think optimistically about yourself and your future. And share this encouragement with others who may need comfort. Then together, your hearts can rejoice as you praise your Father in heaven and thank Him for His gifts. After all, He has already given you so much . . . and He wants to give you so much more.

There is not one blade of grass, there is no color in this world that is not intended to make us rejoice.
John Calvin

When Behavior Reflects Belief

Teach me, O Lord, the way of Your statutes,
and I shall keep it to the end. Give me understanding,
and I shall keep Your law; indeed,
I shall observe it with my whole heart.
Psalm 119:33–34 NKJV

When we act in accordance with our beliefs—beliefs we've built on the foundation of God's Word—we inevitably feel more comfortable with our decisions. Why? Because we know intuitively, as well as from experience, that sound, biblically based convictions seldom lead us astray.

When you listen carefully to the quiet voice of God deep within your heart, you will make good choices. So as you decide how to respond to ups and downs of daily living, be sure to stop long enough (and early enough) to listen to God's whispered direction. Then put your faith in motion by making sure your words and your actions line up with the principles of your firm faith. You'll then have the comfort of knowing that with God as your Counselor, you can take the next step with confidence.

One of the ways God
has revealed Himself to us is in the conscience.
Conscience is God's lamp within the human breast.
Billy Graham

Rejoice!

Rejoice in the Lord always. Again I will say, rejoice!
Philippians 4:4 NKJV

Have you made the choice to rejoice? Do you seek happiness, comfort, and contentment? The way to find all of those things is to rejoice—after all, your life is a gift from God, a blessing to be savored and celebrated. And the best day to begin that celebration is this one.

What does life have in store for you? A world full of possibilities (if you'll have faith enough to embrace them) and God's promise of peace and joy (if you'll trust Him enough to accept them). So as you embark upon the next phase of your journey, remember to celebrate the life God has given you. Your Creator has blessed you beyond measure. Honor Him with your prayers, your words, your deeds, and your joy.

The spiritual life is a life beyond moods.
It is a life in which we choose joy and do not allow ourselves to become victims of passing feelings of happiness or depression.
Henri Nouwen

The Anchor

We have this [hope]–like a sure and firm anchor of the soul–that enters the inner sanctuary behind the curtain.

Hebrews 6:19 HCSB

Are you anxious about situations you can't control? Take your anxieties to God. Are you troubled about changes that threaten to disrupt your life? Take your troubles to the One who never changes. Do you feel as though the ground is trembling beneath your feet? Seek stability by standing on the firm foundation of faith.

The same God who created the universe will protect you and be your sanctuary if you just ask Him to . . . so ask, and then serve Him with willing hands and a trusting heart.

Today and every day, you can rest assured that although the world may change moment by moment, God's love endures–unfathomable and unchanging–forever. Let God's love be the anchor of your soul.

When did God's love for you begin? When He began to be God. When did He begin to be God? Never, for He has always been without beginning and without end, and so He has always loved you from eternity.

Saint Francis of Sales

Knowing and Pleasing God

Here's how we can be sure that we know God in the right way: Keep his commandments.

1 John 2:2–3 MSG

In order to enjoy a deeper relationship with God, we must strive diligently to live in accordance with His commandments. But there's a problem—we live in a world that seeks to snare our attention and lead us away from the Creator.

Because we are imperfect beings, we cannot be perfectly obedient, nor does God expect us to be. What He does want and deserve, however, is our sincere desire to please Him and to follow Him.

Are you willing to conform your behavior to God's rules? If you can answer that question with a resounding yes, God will use you and bless you—today, tomorrow, and every day of your life.

Obedience is a foundational stepping-stone on the path of God's Will.

Elizabeth George

Finding Inspiration at Church

We are God's fellow workers; you are God's field, you are God's building.

1 Corinthians 3:9 NKJV

Your church isn't just a place to find God. It's also a place to find inspiration, fellowship, purpose, and comfort. If you'd like to discover these things, a church is a wonderful place to do it.

The church belongs to God; it is His just as certainly as we are His. When we help build God's church, we bear witness to the changes He has made in our lives.

Today and every day, let us worship God with grateful hearts and helping hands as we support the church He has created. Let us share our faith with our friends, our families, and the world. When we do, we'll bless others—and we'll be blessed by the One who sent His Son to bring transformation to our lives and our world.

Make your church grow: some assembly required.

Church sign

Finding Contentment

I've found the recipe for being happy
whether full or hungry, hands full or hands empty.
Philippians 4:12 MSG

Where can we find contentment? Is it a result of wealth or power or beauty or fame? Hardly. Genuine contentment is a gift from God to those who trust Him and follow His commandments.

Our world seems preoccupied with the search for happiness. We're bombarded with messages claiming that happiness hinges on the acquisition of material possessions and creature comforts. But these claims are false. Enduring peace is not the result of what we own; it's a spiritual gift from God to those who obey Him and trust Him enough to accept His will.

If we don't find contentment in God, we'll never find it anywhere else. But if we seek Him, obey Him, and trust Him, we'll be blessed with a level of inner peace that defies human understanding. When we make God the center of our lives, peace and contentment will belong to us just as surely as we belong to God.

He is rich that is satisfied.
Thomas Fuller

Ask and Receive

Ask, and it will be given to you; seek, and you will find;
knock, and it will be opened to you.
For everyone who asks receives, and he who seeks finds,
and to him who knocks it will be opened.
Matthew 7:7–8 NKJV

Jesus told His disciples that they should petition God to meet their needs. But His instruction wasn't just for them—it's for us too. Genuine, heartfelt prayer brings powerful changes in us and in our world. When we lift our hearts to God, we open ourselves to a never-ending source of divine wisdom and infinite love.

Do you have questions about your future? Do you have needs that you simply can't meet by yourself? Do you need comfort? If so, talk to God about it. Ask Him for direction and provision, and to soothe the ache in your heart; keep asking Him for what you need, every day that you live. Whatever you face, pray about it—and never lose hope. God is listening, and He's perfectly capable of answering your prayers. But it's up to you to ask.

God's help is always available,
but it is only given to those who seek it.
Max Lucado

He'll Be There for You

God, who got you started in this spiritual adventure, shares with us the life of his Son and our Master Jesus. He will never give up on you.

1 Corinthians 1:9 MSG

Sometimes the future looks bright, and other times it seems downright daunting. Yet even when we can't see the positive possibilities of tomorrow, God can. Our challenge is to trust an uncertain future to an all-powerful God.

The comforting news is that we can trust Him without reservation. We can steel ourselves against the inevitable disappointments that come our way, secure in the knowledge that our heavenly Father has a plan for the future—a good plan.

Sooner or later, we all confront circumstances that trouble us, even shake us to the core of our souls. That's precisely the moment we need God's comfort—and He will be there for us. So the next time you find your courage stretched to the limit, lean on God's promises. He'll walk with you through life's adventure and He'll never give up on you.

As sure as God puts his children in the furnace he will be in the furnace with them.

C. H. Spurgeon

September 12

Priorities . . . Moment by Moment

You can't go wrong when you love others. When you add up everything in the law code, the sum total is love. But make sure that you don't get so absorbed and exhausted in taking care of all your day-by-day obligations that you lose track of the time and doze off, oblivious to God.

Romans 13:10–11 MSG

Each waking moment holds the potential for you to think a creative thought or offer a heartfelt prayer. So even if you're a person with too many demands and too few hours in which to meet them, take comfort in the knowledge that when you sincerely seek to discover God's priorities for your life, He will provide answers in marvelous and surprising ways.

This is the day God has made, and He has filled it with opportunities to love, to serve, and to seek His guidance. Seize those opportunities. And as a gift to yourself, to your family, and to the world, slow down and take each day moment by moment. You'll soon discover that God's blessings come tucked in the pockets of right priorities.

Putting first things first is an issue at the very heart of life.

Stephen Covey

A Walk with God

Set an example of good works yourself,
with integrity and dignity in your teaching.
Titus 2:7 HCSB

It has been said that character is what we are when nobody is watching. If we sincerely wish to walk with God, we must strive, to the best of our abilities, to follow God's path and to obey His instructions—even when we think no one's looking. In short, we must recognize the importance integrity should play in our lives.

When we listen carefully to God's still, small voice in our hearts, and when we behave in ways that are consistent with His leading, we can't help but receive His blessing.

So today and every day, listen carefully to the Spirit's voice. Build your life on the firm foundation of integrity. When you do, you won't need to look over your shoulder to see who, besides God, is watching.

In matters of style, swim with the current;
In matters of principle, stand like a rock.
Thomas Jefferson

The Gift of Cheerfulness

Worry is a heavy load, but a kind word cheers you up.
Proverbs 12:25 NCV

Cheerfulness is a gift we give to others—and to ourselves. As men and women who have been richly blessed by God, why shouldn't we be cheerful? We have every reason to celebrate our Creator with joy in our hearts, smiles on our faces, and words of praise on our lips.

God promises us lives of joy if we accept His love and His grace and follow His ways. Yet sometimes, even the most righteous fall into the pits of ill temper and frustration. During these moments, we may not feel like turning our thoughts and prayers heavenward, but that's precisely what we must do. Only then can our Helper lighten our load and our hearts. When we commune with our heavenly Father, we simply can't stay grumpy for long. Instead, we'll be able to go out and share a cheerful word with some other heavy heart.

Accept God's gift of cheerfulness . . . and share it with someone today.

So it is with cheerfulness: the more of it is spent,
the more of it remains.
Ralph Waldo Emerson

Comforting Others

A word spoken at the right time is like
golden apples on a silver tray.
Proverbs 25:11 HCSB

Sometimes the world can be a frightening place. At one time or another, most of us will sustain life-altering losses that are so profound and so tragic that it seems we can never recover. But God promises comfort and healing if we'll go to Him. Then, when we have received comfort, we are to comfort others.

When you meet others in need, offer comfort by sharing your courage, your help, and your faith. As the renowned revivalist Vance Havner observed, "No journey is complete that does not lead through some dark valleys. We can properly comfort others only with the comfort wherewith we ourselves have been comforted of God."

Are you in need of comfort today? Discover the miracle of healing that comes when you reach out to comfort others.

Discouraged people don't need critics.
They hurt enough already. They don't need
more guilt or piled-on distress. They need encouragement.
They need a refuge,
a willing, caring, available someone.
Charles Swindoll

Dream Big

A dream fulfilled is a tree of life.
Proverbs 13:12 NLT

Sometimes it's easier to dream than it is to believe in those dreams. We may have high hopes and big plans, but when the storm clouds of life form overhead, it's tempting to give up. Tempting, but potentially tragic. After all, with God as our partner, no challenge is too great, and no mountain is too high.

If you've encountered a setback or two, don't worry too much about your troubles—and never abandon your hopes. Instead, focus on your dreams.

Dreams do come true, and good things do happen to good people. But the best things are usually reserved for those who expect the best, plan for it, and take steps toward achieving it. So think optimistically about your future and your life. Start dreaming big today.

The future belongs to those who believe
in the beauty of their dreams.
Eleanor Roosevelt

Courtesy Matters

Out of respect for Christ,
be courteously reverent to one another.
Ephesians 5:21 MSG

Does the Bible instruct us in matters of etiquette and courtesy? It may surprise you to know that it does. The apostle Paul wrote that we should be "courteously reverent to one another." And Jesus said, "In everything, therefore, treat people the same way you want them to treat you" (Matthew 7:12 NASB). Jesus did not say, "In some things, treat people as you wish to be treated." And He did not say, "From time to time, treat others with kindness." Jesus said that we should treat others as we wish to be treated in every aspect of our daily lives. This is a tall order indeed, but we are commanded to do our best.

Today, consider all the kind things God has done for you, and honor Him by being a little kinder than usual to family members, friends, and even total strangers. Your kindness will not go unnoticed . . . more often than not, it will be returned.

Life be not so short but that there is
always time for courtesy.
Ralph Waldo Emerson

Discipline Yourself

Discipline yourself for the purpose of godliness.
1 Timothy 4:7 NASB

Are you a self-disciplined person? If so, your disciplined approach to life can help you build a more meaningful relationship with God. How can that be? Because God expects all of His followers to lead lives of disciplined obedience to Him . . . and He rewards those who do.

Sometimes it's hard to be disciplined. But persevere: self-discipline never goes out of style, and it will be rewarded.

Your greatest accomplishments in life will probably require plenty of work and a heaping helping of self-discipline—which, by the way, is in line with God's plan. After all, He has promised to give you the strength and to walk with you all along the way. He has big plans for you, and He'll do His part to fulfill those plans. Will you do yours?

If one examines the secret behind a championship football team, a magnificent orchestra,
or a successful business, the principal ingredient is invariably discipline.
James Dobson

Pats on the Back

Let us try to do what makes peace and helps one another.

Romans 14:19 NCV

Life is a team sport, and all of us need occasional pats on the back from our teammates. In the book of Ephesians, Paul wrote, "Do not let any unwholesome talk come out of your mouths, but only what is helpful for building others up according to their needs, that it may benefit those who listen" (4:29 NIV). Paul reminds us that when we choose our words carefully, we can have a powerful impact on those around us.

Since we don't always know who needs our help, the best strategy is to encourage all of the people who cross our paths. So today, be quick to share a kind word, a smile, or a hug. Do your best to be a world-class source of encouragement to everyone you meet. Never has the need been greater.

A single word, if spoken in a friendly spirit,
may be sufficient to turn one from dangerous error.

Fanny Crosby

Enthusiastic Service

Do your work with enthusiasm.
Work as if you were serving the Lord,
not as if you were serving only men and women.
Ephesians 6:7 NCV

This day, like every day, should be cause for celebration. After all, God is good, and His blessings are too numerous to count. In response to the Creator's gifts, we are wise to serve Him with fervor and enthusiasm.

Do you see each day as a glorious opportunity to serve God and to do His will? Are you excited about God's gifts and your own future? Or do you struggle through each day giving scarcely a thought to His blessings? The answer to these questions will have a profound impact on the quality of your thoughts and the direction of your life.

You are the recipient of Christ's sacrificial love. Accept it enthusiastically and share it freely. God deserves your enthusiasm; the world needs it; and you'll be blessed by the experience of sharing it.

Each day I look for a kernel of excitement.
Barbara Jordan

Trusting God's Plan

"My thoughts are not your thoughts, nor are your ways My ways," says the Lord. "For as the heavens are higher than the earth, so are My ways higher than your ways, and My thoughts than your thoughts."

Isaiah 55:8–9 NKJV

Pearl Bailey's singing career spanned six decades, and in 1988 she received a Presidential Medal of Freedom. Bailey explained her success this way: "I never really look for anything. . . . I wake up in the morning and whichever way God turns my feet, I go."

If you've been micromanaging your own life and getting, at best, mixed results, maybe it's time to take Pearl's pearl of wisdom and let God lead the way. When you do, you'll discover that God usually has bigger, better plans than you could possibly envision. So when in doubt, do your best and trust God with the rest. You can confidently entrust your path to Him. When you place your life in God's hands, your future is secure.

Mark it down: things do not "just happen." There is a God-arranged plan for this world of ours, which includes a specific plan for you.

Charles Swindoll

September 22

Family Planning

Love is patient, love is kind and is not jealous; love does not brag and is not arrogant, does not act unbecomingly; it does not seek its own, is not provoked, does not take into account a wrong suffered, does not rejoice in unrighteousness, but rejoices with the truth; bears all things, believes all things, hopes all things, endures all things.

1 Corinthians 13:4–7 NASB

As you make plans for your life, don't forget to consider how those plans will affect the most important people God has entrusted to your care–your family. God intends that we honor Him by honoring our families–by giving them our love, support, advice, cooperation, and, when needed, discipline. But there's no getting around it: these matters require significant investments of time.

God has a plan for your life and a purpose only you can fulfill–a crucial part of the plan–is the comfort, support, and love you give to your family. With a family, God has entrusted you with an important responsibility. They need you, and you need them. But the love of a family is both a comfort and a reward worthy of investment.

Whole-life stewardship means putting the purposes of God at the very center of our lives and families.

Tom Sine

Being Comfortable with Your Finances

Trust in your money and down you go!
But the godly flourish like leaves in spring.
Proverbs 11:28 NLT

From time to time, most of us struggle with money—both how to get it and how to spend it. Sometimes our financial struggles are simply manifestations of the inner conflict we feel when we stray from God's plan.

God doesn't intend for us to keep acquiring more and more stuff. Instead, His Word teaches us to be levelheaded, moderate, and thoughtful about the way we spend the money He entrusts to our care. Today, promise that you'll do whatever it takes to create a sensible financial plan and stick to it. Know where your money is coming from and where it's going. When you become comfortable with your finances, you'll become more comfortable with every other aspect of your life.

That man is rich whose pleasures are the cheapest.
Henry David Thoreau

Fear of Rejection

My dear friends, don't let public opinion influence how you live out our glorious, Christ-originated faith.
James 2:1 MSG

The fear of rejection and its cousin, the fear of failure, are roadblocks on the way to happiness. When we try to please everyone in sight, we create for ourselves a task that is unrealistic, unsatisfying, and unworthy of our efforts.

If you're letting the opinions of others hold too much sway in your life, it's time to start thinking more rationally and faithfully. Remember, your worth comes from God, not public opinion. Sure, there are a few people you should seek to please, like your family, close friends, and the person who signs your paycheck. But trying to please everyone is impossible, and it's not even what God expects—especially when it comes to choosing between people pleasing and keeping the faith. Your top priority should be to please your heavenly Father. Then, even if others reject you, He will accept you and reward you with eternal life.

How far would Moses have gone
if he had taken a poll in Egypt?
Harry S. Truman

The Seeds of Generosity

Freely you have received, freely give.

Matthew 10:8 NIV

It's not complicated: input determines output. What you sow determines what you'll reap. So if you want to enjoy a generous life, sow seeds of generosity.

The thread of generosity is woven into the fabric of Christ's teachings. As He sent His disciples out to heal the sick and spread God's message of salvation, Jesus offered this guiding principle: "Freely you have received, freely give." That principle still applies.

So if you'd like to experience more of God's abundance, try sharing more of it. Generosity isn't restricted to material things, either. Do you seek God's comfort and His peace? Then comfort those around you. Share your possessions, yes. But also share your faith and your love. When you plant the seeds of generosity in others, you'll find you reap an even more bountiful harvest in return.

Abundant living means abundant giving.

E. Stanley Jones

His Comforting Hand

God, who comforts the downcast, comforted us.
2 Corinthians 7:6 NIV

God comforts all who reach out to Him. When we're feeling discouraged, worried, lonely, or afraid, we can call on our heavenly Father in prayer and He will respond to our concerns.

Sometimes God responds by filling our spirits with a sense of peace, a calm that only He can provide. Sometimes He uses our friends and family members to comfort us. And sometimes God performs miracles in our lives, transforming our defeats into victories and our failures into triumphs.

God's response to our needs is varied, but we need never doubt that He will respond in the way He knows is best. When we reach out to God, He reaches back with His comforting hand. When we ask, He answers. He knows our needs, and He knows how best to provide for us. We need only ask, trust, and accept His comfort and His love.

Put your hand into the hand of God.
He gives the calmness and serenity of
heart and soul.
Lettie B. Cowman

Today's Opportunities to Encourage

Encourage each other daily, while it is still called today, so that none of you is hardened by sin's deception.
Hebrews 3:13 HCSB

Each day brings with it opportunities to encourage others and to commend their good works. When we do, we spread seeds of joy and happiness.

God grants each of us the gift of life, and He asks us to celebrate the lives we've been given. One important part of each day's celebration is the time we spend celebrating others. And how best can we celebrate others? By honoring their accomplishments, by rejoicing in their victories, and by recognizing their efforts. But it doesn't stop there. People also need our unconditional encouragement–some heartening words regardless of whether they've been successful in their efforts today. They need encouragement simply regarding who they are, not what they've done.

Today, be slow to criticize and quick to encourage. When you do, you'll be a powerful force for good in the world . . . and for God.

If someone listens or stretches out a hand or whispers a word of encouragement or attempts to understand a lonely person, extraordinary things begin to happen.
Loretta Girzartis

Expecting the Best

This is the day the Lord has made;
let us rejoice and be glad in it.
Psalm 118:24 NIV

What do you expect from the day ahead? Are you anticipating the wonderful things God will do, or are you living under a cloud of apprehension and doubt? The familiar words of Psalm 118:24 remind us that each day should be a cause for celebration. After all, God blesses us abundantly, every day of our lives. He gives us love and assurance. He gives us comfort when we're hurting. And, most important, God promises us the priceless gift of eternal life. As we consider these blessings, our hearts can rejoice and be truly glad.

Daily life brings challenges, it's true. But when we arm ourselves with the promises of God's Word, we can expect the best—not only for the day ahead, but for all eternity.

Each day, each moment is so pregnant
with eternity that if we "tune in" to it,
we can hardly contain the joy.
Gloria Gaither

Reaching Out

Don't be obsessed with getting your own advantage. Forget yourselves long enough to lend a helping hand.
Philippians 2:4 MSG

Noted American theologian Phillips Brooks once advised, "Be such a man, and live such a life, that if every man were such as you, and every life a life like yours, this earth would be God's Paradise."

Sometimes, when we feel happy or generous, we find it easy to do good. Other times, when we're discouraged or weary, we can scarcely summon the energy to utter a single kind word. But the instruction in God's Word is clear: we are to think of others and help them rather than always focusing on our own wants and needs.

Today, consider all the things God has done for you. Forget for a moment about what you want, and reach out to help someone in need. You'll find it brings an even better reward than when you're only looking out for yourself.

It is one of the most beautiful compensations of life that no one can sincerely try to help another without helping herself.
Barbara Johnson

Neighbors in Need

Each one of us needs to look after the good of the people around us, asking ourselves, "How can I help?" That's exactly what Jesus did.

Romans 15:2–3 MSG

Neighbors. We know that we are to love them, and yet there's so little time . . . and we're so busy. No matter. Our Lord and Savior Jesus Christ has commissioned us to love our neighbors just as we love ourselves. Let's face it—that's a lot.

This very day, you will encounter someone who needs a word of comfort, a pat on the back, a helping hand, or a heartfelt prayer. And in the rush and press of your busy day, it's easy to say you don't have time. But stop for just a moment and consider this: If you don't reach out to your friend, who will? If you don't take the time to understand the needs of your neighbors, who will? If you don't love your brothers and sisters, who will?

Today, look for a neighbor in need . . . and then ask, "How can I help?"

We can't help everyone,
but everyone can help someone.

Loretta Scott

October

Honesty with Yourself

Good people will be guided by honesty.
Proverbs 11:3 NCV

Honesty is important and that includes being honest with ourselves. But because we view the world through the subjective lenses of our own particular attitudes and beliefs, it's often hard to be objective about our behaviors, our strengths, our weaknesses, and our motivations.

Do you take the time to honestly assess yourself: to assess the way you typically think and the way you typically behave? Honest self-evaluation is the foundation of lasting self-improvement. And honest self-evaluation can help you become more comfortable with who you are and who you want to become. So don't be afraid to look in the mirror and be honest about (and with) the person you see there. Don't be too hard on yourself, but do look for ways to improve . . . and then get started. Honestly, the person in the mirror will be glad you did.

It isn't until you come to a spiritual understanding of who you are–deep down, the spirit within– that you can begin to take control.
Oprah Winfrey

Laugh!

A happy heart makes the face cheerful.
Proverbs 15:13 NIV

Laughter is God's gift, and He intends for us to enjoy it. Yet sometimes, because of the inevitable stresses of everyday life, laughter seems only a distant memory.

As thoughtful adults, we have every reason to be cheerful and to be thankful. Our blessings from God are beyond measure. So why do we trudge through life with frowns on our faces and in our hearts? Few things in life are more displeasing than the sight of a man or woman grumpily complaining about everything in sight. And few things are more uplifting than the sight of a cheerful man or woman smiling and laughing through life.

Today, as you go about your daily activities, approach life with a grin and a chuckle. After all, God created laughter for a reason . . . so laugh!

Laughter is an instant vacation!
Milton Berle

Mentors That Matter

The lips of the righteous feed many.
Proverbs 10:21 HCSB

Here's a simple yet effective way to improve your life: choose role models whom you admire, and do your best to follow the good examples they set. When you do, you'll become a stronger person as you grow spiritually and emotionally.

Today, as a gift to yourself, select from your friends and family members a godly mentor whose judgment you trust. Then listen carefully to his or her advice—and be willing to accept that advice, even if following it requires effort or even some discomfort.

Whether we're fifteen or ninety-five, we still have lots to learn—and a mentor can help us learn it. Consider your mentor one of God's gifts to you. Thank Him for that gift, and use it for His glory.

Do not open your heart to every man,
but discuss your affairs with one who is wise
and who fears God.
Thomas à Kempis

October 4

Blessed Obedience

When you and your children return to the Lord your God and obey him with all your heart and with all your soul according to everything I command you today, then the Lord your God will restore your fortunes and have compassion on you and gather you again from all the nations where he scattered you.

Deuteronomy 30:2–3 NIV

We live in a world filled with temptations, distractions, and countless opportunities to wander far from the path God has laid out for us. But as men and women who seek to be positive role models for our families, we must turn our thoughts and our hearts away from the temptations and distractions around us. We must turn instead to God, seeking His counsel often—and trusting and following the counsel He gives.

When we invite God to rule over our hearts and our lives, our obedience will bring with it blessing. So today and every day, vow to live according to God's rules, not the world's rules. The world may lead you astray, but God never will. You're safe with Him.

Believe and do what God says. The life-changing consequences will be limitless, and the results will be confidence and peace of mind.

Franklin Graham

Never Give In

We are hard-pressed on every side, yet not crushed;
we are perplexed, but not in despair.
2 Corinthians 4:8 NKJV

A well-lived life calls for preparation, determination, and lots of perseverance. For an example of perfect perseverance, we need look no further than the life of Jesus. The carpenter from Nazareth finished what He started.

Despite His suffering, despite the shame of the cross, Jesus was steadfast in His faithfulness to God. He never gave up and He never gave in. We, too, must remain faithful, especially during times of hardship. Sometimes it seems our prayers meet only with silence; yet even then we must patiently persevere, knowing that God is indeed listening and working on our behalf.

Are you facing a tough situation? A perplexing dilemma? A heartbreaking disappointment? If so, remember this: never give in; whatever your problem, God is willing and able to see you through.

Never give in, Never give in, Never; never;
never; never–in nothing, great or small, large or petty–
never give in except to conviction
of honor and good sense.
Winston Churchill

The Capacity to Forgive

Smart people know how to hold their tongue; their grandeur is to forgive and forget.

Proverbs 19:11 MSG

Martin Luther King Jr. became the symbol of strength and dignity for blacks in America during the turbulent 1960s. And as an acknowledgment of his role in the fight for freedom, he received the Nobel Peace Prize in 1964.

It was King who said, "We must develop and maintain the capacity to forgive." Great advice, but forgiveness is easier said than done. Sometimes we have to work at it for years, trying to forgive those who have hurt us while trying to make peace with the past.

Forgiveness is seldom easy, but it's always worthwhile. We're closer to our Creator when we turn the other cheek: that was the opinion of Dr. King, a man who moved many mountains on the way to his mountaintop.

One of the most time-consuming things is to have an enemy.

E. B. White

The Miracle Worker

You are the God who performs miracles;
you display your power among the peoples.
Psalm 77:14 NIV

God is a miracle worker. Throughout history, He has intervened in the course of human events in ways that cannot be explained by science or by human rationale. And He's still doing so today.

God's miracles are not limited to special occasions, nor are they witnessed only by a select few. God displays His wonders all around us: the miracle of a newborn baby; the miracle of a world renewing itself with every sunrise; the miracle of lives transformed by God's love and grace. Each day, God's handiwork is evident for all to see and experience.

Today, seize the opportunity to see God's hand at work. His miracles come in a variety of shapes and sizes, so keep your eyes and your heart open. Be watchful, and you'll soon be amazed.

Too many times we miss so much because
we live on the low level of the natural,
the ordinary, the explainable.
Vance Havner

A Passionate Life

Never be lacking in zeal, but keep your spiritual fervor, serving the Lord.
Romans 12:11 NIV

Are you passionate about your life, your loved ones, your work, and your faith? If you're a person who trusts God's promises, you have much more cause to be passionate. After all, God's Word tells us we have every reason to be enthusiastic about life here on earth—and the life hereafter. But sometimes the messy struggles of life can leave us feeling decidedly unenthusiastic.

If you feel that your passion for life is slowly fading away, maybe now's the time to slow down, to rest, to count your blessings, and to pray. When you feel worried or weary, fervently petition God to renew your sense of wonder and excitement.

Life with God is a glorious adventure; revel in it. As long as you're alive, live passionately.

Heat is required to forge anything.
Every great accomplishment is
the story of a flaming heart.
Mary Lou Retton

Problems in Perspective

It's important to look at things from God's point of view.
1 Corinthians 4:6 MSG

If a temporary loss of perspective has you worried, exhausted, or both, it's time to readjust your thought patterns. Negative thoughts are habit-forming; fortunately, so are positive ones. With practice you can form the habit of focusing on God's priorities and your possibilities. When you do, you'll soon be spending less time fretting about your challenges and more time praising God for His blessings.

When you call upon the Lord and prayerfully seek His will, He will give you comfort, wisdom, and perspective. When you make God's priorities your priorities, He will direct your steps and calm your fears. So beginning today, pray for a sense of balance and perspective. And remember that no problems are too big for God.

Problems are only opportunities in work clothes.
Henry Kaiser

Keeping Prosperity in Perspective

No one can serve two masters; for either he will hate the one and love the other, or else he will be loyal to the one and despise the other. You cannot serve God and mammon.

Matthew 6:24 NKJV

We live in an era of prosperity, a time when many of us have been richly blessed with an assortment of material possessions that our forebears could scarcely have imagined. As people of faith living in these prosperous times, we must be cautious; we must keep prosperity in perspective.

The world stresses the importance of material possessions; God emphasizes spiritual treasures. The world offers the promise of happiness through wealth and public acclaim; God offers the promise of peace through His Son. Which will you choose?

The world often makes promises it cannot keep, but when God makes a promise, He keeps it—not just for a day or a year or a lifetime, but for all eternity.

Great wealth is not related to money! It is an attitude of satisfaction coupled with inner peace.

Charles Swindoll

Words of Wisdom

The wise don't tell everything they know,
but the foolish talk too much and are ruined.
Proverbs 10:14 NCV

All too often, in the rush to be heard, we speak first and think after . . . with unfortunate results. God's Word reminds us: "Reckless words pierce like a sword, but the tongue of the wise brings healing" (Proverbs 12:18 NIV). If we want to be a source of encouragement to friends and family, then we must measure our words carefully. Words are important: they can hurt or heal. Words can comfort us or discourage us–and reckless words, spoken in haste, cannot be erased.

Today, measure your words carefully. Use words of kindness and praise, not words of anger or derision. Remember that you have the power to bring healing to others or to injure them, to lift others up or to hold them back. When you lift them up, you'll bring healing and comfort to a world that needs both.

A little kindly advice is better than
a great deal of scolding.
Fanny Crosby

October 12

Doers of the Word

Prove yourselves doers of the word, and not merely hearers.
James 1:22 NASB

The old saying is both familiar and true: actions speak louder than words. So our actions should always give testimony to the positive changes God can make in the lives of those who walk with Him.

God calls upon each of us to act in accordance with His will and with respect for His commandments. If we are to be faithful followers of our heavenly Father, we must realize that it's never enough simply to hear His instructions; we must also live by them. And it is never enough to wait idly by while others do good works; we, too, must act. Doing God's work is a responsibility each of us must bear. But when we do, our loving heavenly Father will reward our efforts with a bountiful harvest.

He who waits until circumstances completely favor his undertaking will never accomplish anything.
Martin Luther

The Abundant Life

I came that they may have life, and have it abundantly.

John 10:10 NASB

In John 10:10, the Bible gives us hope—we are told that abundance and contentment can be ours. But what, exactly, did Jesus mean when He promised abundant life? Was He referring to material possessions or financial wealth? Actually, He was talking about much more than that. Jesus was describing a different kind of abundance: a spiritual richness that extends beyond the temporal boundaries of this world.

Is material abundance part of God's plan for our lives? Perhaps. But in every circumstance of life, whether in times of wealth or times of want, God will provide us whatever we need if we trust Him. May we, as children of God, accept His abundance with open arms and open hearts. And may we share His blessings with all who cross our paths.

God loves you and wants you to experience peace and life—abundant and eternal.

Billy Graham

One Mouth, Two Ears, Lots of Encouragement

Everyone should be quick to listen, slow to speak and slow to become angry, for man's anger does not bring about the righteous life that God desires.

James 1:19–20 NIV

God's Word instructs us to be quick to listen and slow to speak. And when it comes to the important job of encouraging our friends and family members, we're wise to listen carefully (first) and then offer helpful words (second).

Perhaps God gave us two ears and one mouth for a reason—so that we might listen twice as much as we speak. After all, listening quietly to another person can sometimes be a wonderful form of encouragement. Besides, after you've listened carefully to the other guy (or gal), you're more likely to speak wisely rather than impulsively.

Today and every day, you have the power to comfort others with your words *and* your ears . . . with an emphasis on the latter. Sometimes the words you *don't* speak are just as comforting as the ones you *do* speak.

The battle of the tongue is won not in the mouth, but in the heart.

Annie Chapman

Looking Forward with Hope

If we look forward to something we don't yet have,
we must wait patiently and confidently.
Romans 8:25 NLT

At a college track meet, one young man set three world records in under an hour. As an Olympian, he humiliated Adolph Hitler by winning four gold medals in the 1936 Summer Olympics in Berlin. The man was Jesse Owens—grandson of slaves, son of an Alabama sharecropper; and one of the greatest athletes of the twentieth century.

Owens was, by nature, an optimist. He said, "Find the good. It's all around you. Find it, showcase it, and you'll start believing in it."

The next time you find yourself caught up in the rat race, remember Jesse Owens. Look for the good, expect the best, and set about pursuing your dreams. When you look through eyes of hope, you can look forward with confidence.

Never yield to gloomy anticipation.
Place your hope and confidence in God.
He has no record of failure.
Lettie B. Cowman

What Doesn't Change

Unfailing love surrounds those who trust the Lord.
Psalm 32:10 NLT

Every day we encounter a multitude of changes—some good, some not so good, some downright disheartening. On those occasions when we must endure devastating personal losses that leave us stunned and seemingly unable to move, there is someone we can turn to for comfort and assurance: we can turn to God. When we do, our loving heavenly Father stands ready to protect us, to comfort us, to guide us, and, in time, to heal us.

Are you facing an unwelcome change or life-altering setback? If so, don't suffer alone. Turn to God for the ultimate source of comfort. He never changes . . . and He will surround you with His unfailing love.

God carries your picture in his wallet.
Tony Campolo

A Wing and a Prayer

Be cheerful. Keep things in good repair.
Keep your spirits up. Think in harmony. Be agreeable.
Do all that, and the God of love and peace
will be with you for sure.
2 Corinthians 13:11 MSG

We should never underestimate the power of a kind word, a sincere smile, a pat on the back, or a heartfelt hug. And we must never underestimate the importance of cheerfulness. The Bible teaches us that a cheerful heart is like medicine: it makes us (and the people around us) feel better.

Where does cheerfulness begin? It begins on the inside—in our hearts, our thoughts, and our prayers—and works its way out from there.

The world would like you to think that material possessions can bring happiness, but don't believe it. Lasting happiness can't be bought; it's the result of diligent effort in the disciplines of positive thought, heartfelt prayer, and good deeds. But a cheerful heart blessed by God's love and peace is well worth the effort.

Wondrous is the strength of cheerfulness.
Thomas Carlyle

God Is Here

Draw near to God, and He will draw near to you.
James 4:8 HCSB

God is constantly making Himself available to us; so when we approach Him sincerely—with our hearts and minds lifted up to Him in prayer—we can sense His presence and His love. Why, then, does the Creator sometimes seem distant from us . . . or altogether absent? The answer has little to do with God and everything to do with us. When God seems far removed from our lives, it's a result of our own emotional struggles and shortcomings, not an indication of God's absence.

Nobody's perfect and we all have times when we feel far from God. Even though it's usually because we've put the distance between us and Him, that's actually good news. Because anytime we genuinely desire to establish a closer relationship with the Creator, we can do so—all we have to do is draw near to Him. When you do that, He will be right by your side . . . always.

What God promises is that He always, always comes. He always shows up. He always saves. He always rescues. His timing is not ours. His methods are usually unconventional. But what we can know, what we can settle in our soul, is that He is faithful to come when we call.

Angela Thomas

Keep Swinging

In my distress I prayed to the Lord,
and the Lord answered me and set me free.
The Lord is for me, so I will have no fear.
Psalm 118:5–6 NLT

Babe Ruth overcame a troubled childhood to become, perhaps, the greatest figure in the history of baseball. His philosophy at the plate mirrored his outlook on life: swing away, and give it all you've got. So it's no coincidence that the Babe achieved records for both home runs and strikeouts.

Ruth once advised, "Never let the fear of striking out get in your way." And that's smart play on the diamond or off. So the next time you're facing a tough pitch, think of a poor boy who grew up on the wrong side of the tracks, but kept swinging until he slugged his way into the Hall of Fame. And don't worry about a few strikeouts, because there's always another at bat for people (like you) who simply won't stop swinging.

Only those who dare to fail greatly
can ever achieve greatly.
Robert Kennedy

Hope

The lines of purpose in your lives never grow slack,
tightly tied as they are to your future in heaven,
kept taut by hope.
Colossians 1:5 MSG

While she was only in her twenties, Emily Dickinson withdrew from society. But the young woman was certainly not idle. She wrote poetry, some of the finest American poems ever penned. After her death, more than 1,700 of those poems were discovered, and her words continue to move readers even today.

Dickinson wrote, "Hope is the thing with feathers that perches in the soul." What a wonderful portrayal of that mysterious, miraculous feeling. Our hopes feed our souls.

Sometimes when life seems to fly out of control, it's easy to lose hope. But don't let the thing with feathers fly away. If you find yourself giving in to the twin evils of pessimism and doubt, please reconsider. As Emily Dickinson would be quick to point out, hope is powerful medicine for the soul. Make it your medicine.

What oxygen is to the lungs,
such is hope to the meaning of life.
Emil Brunner

Secure in His Love

The faithful love of the Lord never ends!
Lamentations 3:22 NLT

We live in a time of uncertainty and danger, a time when even the most courageous among us have legitimate cause for concern. But we can find comfort in the knowledge that God loves us, that He will guide us, and that He will protect us. When we think carefully and prayerfully about the role God can (and should) play in our lives, we can live courageously, knowing that we are secure in our Father's love.

Are you anxious? Take those anxieties to God. Are you troubled? Take your troubles to Him. Seek protection from the Almighty. And then live courageously knowing that even in these troubled times, you need not fear.

A man who is intimate with God will never be intimated by men.
Leonard Ravenhill

Dealing with Disappointment

We were burdened beyond measure, above strength,
so that we despaired even of life. Yes, we had the sentence
of death in ourselves, that we should not trust in ourselves
but in God who raises the dead, who delivered us from
so great a death, and does deliver us;
in whom we trust that He will still deliver us.
2 Corinthians 1:8–10 NKJV

From time to time, each of us must endure trouble and disappointments that leave us scratching our heads wondering, "Why me?" Often these events come unexpectedly, leaving us with too many questions and not enough answers. Yet even when we don't have all the answers—or, for that matter, when we don't seem to have any of the answers—God does. And since our Creator loves us without condition, we need never give up; we need never give in.

Whatever your circumstances, whether you're standing atop the highest mountain or wandering through the darkest valley, God is with you and will comfort you when you go to him in faith. When you are burdened, He will deliver you.

The best successes come after disappointments.
Henry Ward Beecher

Having Faith

Lord, I believe; help my unbelief!
Mark 9:24 NKJV

Even the most faithful men and women can be overcome by occasional bouts of fear and doubt. When those inevitable fears and doubts begin to grow, what should you do? The answer is straightforward: whenever you feel that your faith is being tested or pushed to its limits, seek the comfort, the assurance, and the love of your heavenly Father.

Even if you feel distant from God, you can be certain that He is never distant from you. To the contrary, He is always with you, always ready to reassure you if you reach out to Him. When you sincerely seek God's presence, He will comfort your heart, calm your fears, and restore your faith in the future . . . and your faith in Him.

We basically have two choices to make
in dealing with the mysteries of God.
We can wrestle with Him or we can rest in Him.
Calvin Miller

Blessing Others

Be agreeable, be sympathetic, be loving, be compassionate, be humble. That goes for all of you, no exceptions. No retaliation. No sharp-tongued sarcasm. Instead, bless–that's your job, to bless.

1 Peter 3:8–9 MSG

As a thoughtful person who's been richly blessed by the Creator, you have every reason to be optimistic about life–and you have every reason to share your hope with others.

Make no mistake: One of the reasons God placed you here on earth is so that you might become a beacon of His light and an encouragement to the world. When you give hope to others, before long they give it to others still . . . and eventually it comes back to you.

As you go about your tasks, celebrate the good that you find in others. As the old saying goes, "When someone does something good, applaud–you'll make two people happy." Give someone a much-needed round of applause today.

There are no words to express the abyss between isolation and having one ally. It may be conceded to the mathematician that four is twice two. But two is not twice one; two is two thousand times one.

G. K. Chesterton

Striving for Significance

The Lord directs the steps of the godly. He delights in every detail of their lives. Though they stumble, they will never fall, for the Lord holds them by the hand.
Psalm 37:23–24 NLT

Sometimes it's easy to look at famous people and presume that their lives have more significance than our own. But if we assume, even for a moment, that our own lives lack significance, we are mistaken. God has a plan for each of us, a direction in which He is leading us, a path of great significance to Him. Our task, simply stated, is to discover, as best we can, what God wants us to do . . . and to do it.

It's comforting to know that when we're following God's path, our lives have ultimate–and eternal–significance. Novelist Willa Cather observed, "Life [hurries] past us . . . , too strong to stop, too sweet to lose." Life indeed hurries, but remember that no matter what stage of life you're in, there is still time to do significant work . . . work that no one but you can do. And the best day to begin that work is today.

It's incredible to realize that what we do each day has meaning in the big picture of God's plan.
Bill Hybels

Choices

Cheerfully pleasing God is the main thing,
and that's what we aim to do,
regardless of our conditions.
2 Corinthians 5:9 MSG

From the instant you wake up in the morning until the moment you nod off to sleep at night, you make lots of decisions: decisions about the things you do, decisions about the words you speak, and decisions about the thoughts you choose to entertain. Simply put, your life is a series of choices—and the choices you make determine the direction and quality of your life.

If you sincerely want to lead a life that is pleasing to your Creator, make daily, moment-by-moment choices that are pleasing to Him. Think carefully—and prayerfully—about your choices. And when in doubt, don't make a move until you've talked things over with God.

In the long run, we shape our lives,
and we shape ourselves. . . . And the choices
we make are ultimately our own responsibility.
Eleanor Roosevelt

Unfulfilled Promises

If you belonged to the world, its people would love you.
But you don't belong to the world.
I have chosen you to leave the world behind.
John 15:19 CEV

The world promises happiness, contentment, love, and abundance. But those are promises it simply cannot fulfill. True love and lasting happiness are not the result of worldly possessions; they're a result of the relationship we choose to have with God. The world's promises are incomplete and illusory; God's promises are unfailing. But to see God's promises fulfilled in our lives, we have to be willing to leave the world behind.

If you've grown weary of the world's unfulfilled promises, tired of looking for love in all the wrong places, take heart. You were not made for the world, and the world will never love you like God does. You were made for close, fulfilling fellowship with Him. So build your life on the firm foundation of God's promises; nothing else even comes close.

Too many Christians have geared their program to please,
to entertain, and to gain favor from
this world. We are concerned with how much, instead of
how little, like this age we can become.
Billy Graham

How to Win Friends

A friend loves you all the time,
and a brother helps in time of trouble.
Proverbs 17:17 NCV

His name remains synonymous with enthusiasm and salesmanship. No wonder. For nearly a century, men and women from all walks of life have attended classes that he designed. These classes teach confidence, motivation, and relationship skills. His name was Dale Carnegie and he was the author of the perennial bestseller *How to Win Friends and Influence People.*

Carnegie had specific advice about friendship. He said, "You can make more friends in two months by becoming more interested in other people than you can in two years by trying to get people interested in you." So if you want to win friends and influence people, take it from the man who wrote the book. Get interested in them, and pretty soon, they'll get interested in you.

A friend may well be reckoned
the masterpiece of nature.
Ralph Waldo Emerson

Light for Today

Lord, You light my lamp;
my God illuminates my darkness.
Psalm 18:28 HCSB

The path to spiritual maturity unfolds day by day. Each day offers the opportunity to worship God, to ignore God, or to rebel against God. When we worship Him with our prayers, our words, our thoughts, and our actions, we'll be blessed by the richness of our relationship with the Father.

In quiet moments when we open our hearts to God, the One who made us keeps remaking us. He gives us direction, perspective, wisdom, and courage.

When it comes to your faith, you won't be "fully grown" in this lifetime. Spiritual maturity is a lifelong journey, but we have the comfort of knowing that God will light the path, one day at a time. God still has important lessons He wants to teach you. Today, ask Him to light your way . . . and then follow where He leads.

God loves us the way we are,
but too much to leave us that way.
Leighton Ford

Great Faithfulness

The Lord is faithful; He will strengthen and guard you.
2 Thessalonians 3:3 HCSB

God is faithful to us . . . even when we are not faithful to Him. God keeps His promises to us even when we stray far from His will. He continues to love us even when we disobey His commandments. But God will not force His blessings upon us. If we are to experience His love and His grace, we must open our hearts to Him and accept them.

Are you tired, discouraged, or fearful? Be comforted: God is with you. Are you confused? Listen to the quiet voice of your heavenly Father. Are you bitter? Talk with God and seek His healing. Are you celebrating a great victory? Thank God and praise Him: He is the Giver of all things good.

In whatever condition you find yourself, trust God and be comforted. He is faithful and He will watch over you and give you the strength you need for today.

God's faithfulness and grace
make the impossible possible.
Sheila Walsh

Always with You

You will show me the way of life,
granting me the joy of your presence
and the pleasures of living with you forever.
Psalm 16:11 NLT

Do you ever wonder if God is really there? If so, you're not the first person to think such thoughts. In fact, some of the grandest heroes in the Bible had their doubts. But when questions arise and doubts begin to creep into your mind, remember this: you take those questions and doubts to God. They don't threaten Him. He already knows your heart and your mind, . . . so why not go to Him and give Him the chance to give you the answers and the faith you seek? He will give you the assurance that He's not only out there–He's right here, with you.

Today, quiet yourself long enough to sense His presence. God will comfort your heart and renew your spirit. He's always with you, willing to show you the way and grant you the pleasures of living with Him forever.

We are never more fulfilled than when our longing for God is met by His presence in our lives.
Billy Graham

November

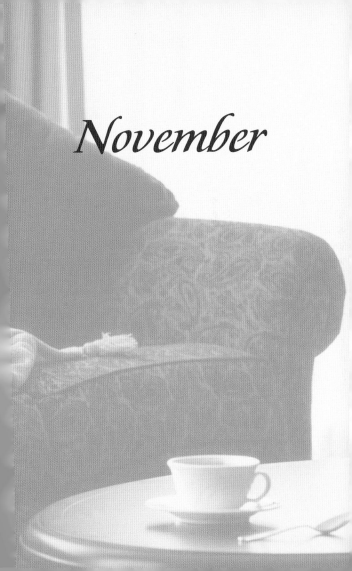

Sufficient for Your Needs

*God is able to make all grace abound toward you,
that you, always having all sufficiency in all things,
may have an abundance for every good work.*
2 Corinthians 9:8 NKJV

God is all-powerful; His love is all-encompassing, timeless, and complete—and it's meant specifically for you.

Of this you can be sure: the love of God is sufficient to meet your needs. Whatever dangers you may face, whatever heartbreaks you must endure, God is with you, and He stands ready to comfort you and to heal you.

If you're experiencing the intense pain of a recent loss, or if you're still mourning a loss from long ago, perhaps today you can begin the next stage of your journey with God. His loving heart is willing, and He is sufficient to meet any challenge, including yours.

*God is, must be, our answer to every question
and every cry of need.*
Hannah Whitall Smith

Being Thankful

Let the peace of God rule in your hearts . . .
and be thankful.
Colossians 3:15 NKJV

For most of us, life is busy and complicated. We're constantly on the go. We have countless responsibilities, some of which begin before sunrise and many of which end long after sunset. So amid the rush and crush of the daily grind, it is easy to lose sight of God and His blessings. But when we forget to slow down and say thank you to our Maker, we rob ourselves of His peace, His joy, and His comfort.

Our task, as thoughtful and thankful adults, is to take the time–to make the time–to praise God many times each day. Then, with gratitude in our hearts, we can face our daily duties with the peace, perspective, and power that only He can provide.

Gratitude changes the pangs of memory into
a tranquil joy.
Dietrich Bonhoeffer

Above and Beyond Our Circumstances

We take the good days from God–
why not also the bad days?
Job 2:10 MSG

All of us face difficult days. When times are tough, even the most optimistic men and women can become discouraged, and you're no exception. After all, you live in a world where expectations can be high and demands can be even higher.

If you become discouraged with the direction of your day–or of your life–turn your thoughts and prayers to your Father in heaven. Focus on His blessings, not on your hardships. Seek His will and follow it. Ask Him to give you strength and expect Him to work miracles. He is a God of possibility, not negativity. He will guide you through your difficulties . . . and beyond them.

The strengthening of faith comes from staying
with it in the hour of trial.
We should not shrink from tests of faith.
Catherine Marshall

Defeating Discouragement

The Lord is the One who will go before you.
He will be with you; He will not leave you or forsake you.
Do not be afraid or discouraged.
Deuteronomy 31:8 HCSB

When we fail to meet the expectations of others (or, for that matter, the expectations we have of ourselves), we may be tempted to abandon hope. But on those cloudy days when our strength is sapped and our faith is shaken, there exists a source from which we can draw courage and wisdom. That source is God.

When we pursue a more intimate and dynamic relationship with our Creator, He renews our spirits and restores our souls. God's promise in Isaiah 40:31 is clear: "Those who wait on the Lord shall renew their strength; they shall mount up with wings like eagles, they shall run and not be weary, they shall walk and not faint" (NKJV). Upon this promise we can depend.

If I am asked how we are to get rid of discouragements, I can only say, as I have had to say of so many other wrong spiritual habits, we must give them up.
It is never worthwhile to argue against discouragement.
There is only one argument that can meet it,
and that is the argument of God.
Hannah Whitall Smith

Thy Will Be Done

"Father, if it is Your will, take this cup away from Me; nevertheless not My will, but Yours, be done."

Luke 22:42 NKJV

When Jesus went to the Mount of Olives, as described in Luke 22, He poured out His heart to God. Jesus knew of the agony that He was destined to endure, but He also knew that God's will must be done. We, like Jesus, may face trials that bring fear and trembling to the depths of our souls, but like Christ, we must seek God's will, not our own.

God has a plan for all our lives, but He will not force His plan on us. To the contrary, He only makes His plans clear to those who genuinely and humbly seek His will. As this day unfolds, let us seek God's will and obey His Word. When we entrust our lives to Him completely and without reservation, He gives us the courage to face any challenge . . . and the peace to live according to His will.

You cannot stay where you are and go with God. You cannot continue doing things your way and accomplish God's purposes in His ways.
Your thinking cannot come close to God's thoughts. For you to do the will of God, you must adjust your life to Him, His purposes, and His ways.

Henry Blackaby

A Good Example

In everything set them an example by doing what is good.

Titus 2:7 NIV

Stephen Covey, author of *The 7 Habits of Highly Effective People*, said: "You cannot not model. It's impossible. People will see your example, positive or negative, as a pattern for the way life is lived." He was right: all of us are role models, whether we intend to be or not.

What kind of example are you? Are you the kind of person whose life serves as a shining example of decency, honesty, and generosity? Are you a person whose behavior serves as a positive role model for others? Are you kind to everyone you meet, no matter his or her station in life? If so, you're a powerful force for good in a world that desperately needs positive influences such as yours–and God will bless you for it.

A holy life will produce the deepest impression. Lighthouses blow no horns; they only shine.

D. L. Moody

Watching Over Your Family

Through your faith God is protecting you by his power until you receive this salvation.

1 Peter 1:5 NLT

These are difficult days for our nation and for our families. But the good news is that God is bigger than all of our problems. God loves us and protects us. In times of trouble, He comforts us; in times of sorrow, He dries our tears. When we are troubled or weak or sorrowful, God is always near, ready to help.

Are you concerned for the well-being of your family? You're not alone. We live in a world where temptations and dangers seem to lurk on every street corner. Parents and children alike have good reason to be watchful. But despite the challenges of our time, God remains steadfast. Even in these difficult days, God is watching over you.

It is easy to love the people far way. It is not always easy to love those close to us. It is easier to give a cup of rice to relieve hunger than to relieve the loneliness and pain of someone unloved in our own home. Bring love into your home for this is where our love for each other must start.

Mother Teresa

Standing Strong

God has not given us a spirit of fear and timidity, but of power, love, and self-discipline.

2 Timothy 1:7 NLT

All of us find our courage tested by the inevitable challenges of life. And when we focus on our fears and our doubts, we find many reasons to lie awake at night and fret about the uncertainties of the future. But here's a better strategy: focus not on your fears but on your God.

Are you willing to trust God, not just when times are good, but also when times are tough? He will be your shield and your strength if you go to Him in faith and trust Him with your life. So the next time you're tempted to accentuate the negative, don't do it. Stand strong and remember that God has not given you a spirit of fear; He gives power and love so you can go on with courage and strength. Trust God's plan and His eternal love for you.

God did away with all my fear. It was time for someone to stand up–or in my case, sit down.
So I refused to move.

Rosa Parks

The Habit of Forgiveness

Be even-tempered, content with second place, quick to forgive an offense. Forgive as quickly and completely as the Master forgave you.

Colossians 3:13 MSG

Have you formed the habit of forgiving everybody (including yourself) as soon as possible? The wise person does just that. But sometimes forgiveness is difficult.

When we've been injured or embarrassed, we feel the urge to strike back and to hurt the ones who have hurt us. But Jesus taught that forgiveness is God's way and that mercy is an integral part of God's plan for our lives. In short, we are commanded to weave the thread of forgiveness into the fabric of our lives.

Have you made forgiveness a high priority? Have you sincerely asked God to forgive you for your unwillingness to forgive others? Have you genuinely prayed that those feelings of hatred and anger might be swept from your heart? If not, do so today . . . it's time to free yourself from the chains of bitterness and regret.

Bitterness imprisons life; love releases it.

Harry Emerson Fosdick

The Shepherd's Care

Your righteousness, O God, reaches to the heavens,
you who have done great things.
Psalm 71:19 NASB

Life isn't easy. Far from it! Sometimes life can be difficult indeed. But even during our darkest moments, we're protected by a loving, heavenly Father.

When we're worried, God can reassure us; when we're sad, God can comfort us. When our hearts are broken, God can bring healing. So we must lift our thoughts and prayers to Him. When we do, He will hear us and answer our prayers.

It's a truth displayed over and over again in the Bible: whatever our problem, God can handle it. He is our shepherd and He has promised to look out for us now and forever. You can trust Him, even on your most difficult days. He has done great things in the past, and the Good Shepherd will do great things in your life if you just follow Him. And why wouldn't you follow? With God at your side, you have nothing to fear.

Cast your cares on God; that anchor holds.
Alfred Lord Tennyson

Blessed Beyond Measure

The Lord bless you and keep you; the Lord make His face shine upon you, and be gracious to you.

Numbers 6:24–25 NKJV

Because we have been so richly blessed, we should make thanksgiving a habit, a regular part of our daily routines. But sometimes, amid the demands and obligations of everyday life, we may allow interruptions and distractions to interfere with that time of thanksgiving—and even take away from the time we spend with God.

Have you counted your blessings today? And have you thanked God for them? Just a few of His many gifts include your family, your friends, your talents, your opportunities, your possessions, and the priceless gift of eternal life. What glorious gifts! And your loving, heavenly Father is the source of every one of them.

So today, as you go about your duties, remember to pause and give thanks to the Lord. He has blessed you beyond measure.

God is the giver, and we are the receivers.
And His richest gifts are bestowed not upon those who do the greatest things, but upon those who accept His abundance and His grace.

Hannah Whitall Smith

Trusting God to Guide You

Trust in the Lord with all your heart and lean not on your own understanding; in all your ways acknowledge him, and he will make your paths straight.

Proverbs 3:5–6 NIV

It's easy to become confused or disoriented by the endless complications and countless distractions of life in the twenty-first century. After all, the world is brimming with them, and if we're not careful, our thoughts and hearts can be hijacked by the negativity that seems to pervade our troubled society.

If you're confused by the complications of everyday life—or if you're unsure of your next step—lean upon God's promises and lift your prayers to Him. Remember that God is your protector. He will love you forever. You are His. Open your heart to Him and trust Him to guide you. When you do, God will direct your steps and you will receive His blessings today, tomorrow, and throughout eternity.

God's grand strategy, birthed in His grace toward us in Christ, and nurtured through the obedience of disciplined faith, is to release us into the redeemed life of our heart, knowing it will lead us back to Him even as the North Star guides a ship across the vast unknown surface of the ocean.

John Eldredge

Ultimate Protection

God is striding ahead of you. He's right there with you.
He won't let you down; he won't leave you.
Don't be intimidated. Don't worry.
Deuteronomy 31:8 MSG

It's undeniable: the world can be a dangerous, unsettling place. But you need not journey through this life alone. God is always with you.

In a world filled with dangers and temptations, God is the ultimate armor. In a world filled with misleading messages, God's Word is the ultimate truth. In a world filled with more frustrations than we can count, God offers the ultimate peace.

God has promised to guide us and to protect us, and He always keeps His promises. Are you willing to trust those promises? Will you accept God's peace and wear God's armor against the dangers of our world? When you do, you'll be empowered to live courageously, knowing that you have the ultimate protection–God's unfailing love for you.

There is no safer place to live than
the center of His will.
Calvin Miller

Waiting for God

*The Lord is good to those who wait for Him,
to the soul who seeks Him. It is good that one should
hope and wait quietly for the salvation of the Lord.*
Lamentations 3:25–26 NKJV

Most of us are impatient for God to grant us the desires of our heart. Usually we know what we want, and we know precisely when we want it—right now, if not sooner. But when God's plans differ from our own, we must trust His infinite wisdom and His infinite love.

As busy men and women living in a fast-paced world, many of us find that waiting quietly for God is difficult. Why? Because we are fallible human beings seeking to live according to our own timetables, not God's. In our better moments, we realize that patience is not only a virtue, but it is also the essence of wisdom and the foundation of trust.

So the next time you find yourself impatient for God to reveal His plans, remember that He loves you and that His timetable is always perfect. And have the wisdom to wait.

*Your times are in His hands.
He's in charge of the timetable, so wait patiently.*
Kay Arthur

God First

Steep your life in God-reality, God-initiative,
God-provisions. Don't worry about missing out.
You'll find all your everyday human concerns will be met.
Matthew 6:33 MSG

One of the quickest—and the surest—ways to improve your day and your life is to make God your partner. When you put God first in every aspect of your life, you'll be comforted by the knowledge that His wisdom is the ultimate wisdom and that His plans are the right plans for you. When you put God first, your outlook will change, your priorities will change, and your behaviors will change. And, when you put Him first, you'll experience the genuine peace and lasting comfort that only He can give.

In the book of Exodus (20:3), God instructs us to place no gods before Him. Does God rule your heart? Make certain that the honest answer to this question is a resounding yes. And then prepare yourself for the cascade of spiritual and emotional blessings that are sure to follow!

Worshipping God begins by recognizing
who God is, His attributes, and how God
expresses Himself in His works.
Franklin Graham

God's Way: Truth

The godly are directed by honesty.

Proverbs 11:5 NLT

From the time we are children, we're taught that honesty is the best policy. Yet sometimes it's difficult for us to be honest with other people, and it can be just as difficult to be honest with ourselves. Nonetheless, even when it's tough to be truthful, we can be comforted by the knowledge that honesty is not just the best policy, it's also God's policy, pure and simple.

When you summon the determination and the courage to be forthright with other folks—and when you are equally honest with yourself—you'll reap the rewards of those efforts. So the next time you're confronted with a situation that offers you the choice between the truth and something less, choose truth. It's the best way to communicate . . . and the best way to live.

God doesn't expect you to be perfect,
but he does insist on complete honesty.

Rick Warren

God's Lessons

Take good counsel and accept correction–
that's the way to live wisely and well.
Proverbs 19:20 MSG

When it comes to learning life's lessons, we can either do things the easy way or the hard way. The easy way can be summed up as follows: when God teaches us a lesson, we learn it . . . the first time. Unfortunately, too many of us learn a little more slowly than that.

When we accept God's instruction early, we avail ourselves of His infinite wisdom, and we are blessed because of our willingness to let God lead the way. Our challenge, of course, is to do our best to discern God's lessons in the experiences of everyday life.

Today, determine to learn those lessons sooner rather than later–because the sooner you do, the sooner God can lead you onward and upward to the next lesson, and the next, and the next . . .

Learning is not attained by chance,
it must be sought for with ardor
and attended to with diligence.
Abigail Adams

The Right Kind of Riches

Love not the world, neither the things that are in the world. If any man love the world, the love of the Father is not in him.
1 John 2:15 KJV

Okay, be honest—are you just a little bit in love with stuff? Or maybe a whole lot in love, and your pursuit of possessions has left you feeling empty? If so, you know the painful truth that no matter how much you love stuff, stuff won't love you back.

Material goods are not nearly as important as we sometimes make them out to be. Of course, we all need the basic necessities of life; however, once we meet those needs for ourselves and our families, the piling up of possessions often creates more problems than it solves. But God has promised us riches far beyond those of this world. When we love Him, He loves us back—and we become rich in spirit.

Martin Luther observed, "Many things I have tried to grasp and have lost. That which I have placed in God's hands I still possess." Although our earthly riches are transitory, we can store up spiritual riches that will last forever.

When we put people before possessions in our hearts, we are sowing seeds of enduring satisfaction.
Beverly LaHaye

Looking for the Good

Make me hear joy and gladness.
Psalm 51:8 NKJV

If you believe in an all-knowing, all-loving God, you'll find it hard to be a pessimist. After all, with God in His heaven—and on your side—you have every reason to have a positive outlook. Yet you're only human, so from time to time you may fall prey to fear, doubt, or discouragement. If you've been plagued by these negative feelings lately, it's time to lift your hopes . . . and lift a few prayers to God.

Time and again, the Bible reminds us of God's blessings. In response to His grace, let us strive to focus our thoughts on things that are pleasing to Him, not upon things that are corrupting, discouraging, or frustrating.

The next time you find yourself mired in the pit of pessimism, ask God to help you redirect your thoughts. Ask Him to make you hear joy and gladness. This world is God's wonderful creation; when you look to Him and look for the best, you won't have to look far to find it.

There is wisdom in the habit of looking
at the bright side of life.
Father Flanagan

Real Repentance

I preached that they should repent and turn to God and prove their repentance by their deeds.
Acts 26:20 NIV

Who among us has sinned? All of us. But the good news is this: when we sincerely turn our hearts to God and ask Him to forgive us, He does forgive–absolutely and completely.

Genuine repentance requires more than simply offering God apologies for our misdeeds. Real repentance may start with feelings of sorrow and remorse, but it ends only when we turn away from the sin that has heretofore distanced us from our Creator. We offer our most meaningful apologies to God not with our words, but with our actions. As long as we are still engaged in wrong behaviors, we may be "repenting," but we have not fully "repented."

Is some aspect of your life distancing you from God? Real repentance may not be easy, but you don't have to do even that much alone. When you ask God to forgive you, ask Him also to help you to live out your repentance by changing your behavior. He will be faithful to strengthen you . . . and to draw you back into His loving arms.

To do so no more is the truest repentance.
Martin Luther

Remaining Humble

When you do things, do not let selfishness or pride be your guide. Instead, be humble and give more honor to others than to yourselves.

Philippians 2:3 NCV

Humility earns rewards that pride will never know. That's why the greatest people are those humble servants who care little for their own glory and choose, instead, to give God the credit He deserves.

Sometimes our faith is tested more by prosperity than by adversity. Why? Because in times of plenty we may be tempted to convince ourselves (wrongly) that we're "self-made" men and women. In truth, all of our gifts flow from the Creator.

Would you like to experience the full measure of God's blessings? To experience the peace and comfort that accrue to the most humble of God's servants? Then give the Father the full measure of your thanksgiving, with humility in your heart and praise on your lips–starting now.

A man wrapped up in himself makes a very small bundle.

Ben Franklin

Seek, Find, and Ask

If you seek God, your God, you'll be able to find him
if you're serious, looking for him
with your whole heart and soul.
Deuteronomy 4:29 MSG

Where is God? He is everywhere you have ever been and everywhere you will ever go. He is with you night and day; He knows your every thought; He hears your every heartbeat. But sometimes, in the crush of your daily duties, God may seem far away. Or when the disappointments and sorrows of life leave you brokenhearted, you can feel as thought God is distant—but He's not. When you earnestly seek God, you will find Him. He wants you to seek Him; He wants to be found by you. He is right here, waiting patiently for you to reach out to Him.

Would you like to experience the comfort, the peace, and the assurance that only God can give? Then send your soul on a God quest. When you seek Him with all your heart, He will not hide from you; He will show Himself in real and wonderful ways.

Don't take anyone else's word for God.
Find him for yourself, and then you, too, will know, by the wonderful, warm tug on your heartstrings, that he is there for sure.
Billy Graham

Cause to Celebrate

A miserable heart means a miserable life;
a cheerful heart fills the day with song.
Proverbs 15:15 MSG

Life should be a cause for celebration, but sometimes we don't feel much like celebrating. In fact, when the weight of the world seems to bear down upon our shoulders, celebration may be the last thing on our minds . . . but it shouldn't be. This day is a precious gift, but it expires at the stroke of midnight. So let us give thanks for these hours on loan from heaven, celebrating them and filling them with song.

God created you in His own image, and He wants you to experience joy and abundance. And He will do His part to ensure that you know spiritual peace and comfort. His love and the life He has given you are ample reason to celebrate. Today, refuse to give in to misery. Choose a cheerful heart, for God has given you plentiful cause to celebrate.

You've heard the saying, "Life is what you make it." That means we have a choice. We can choose to have a life full of frustration and fear, but we can just as easily choose one of joy and contentment.

Dennis Swanberg

Refining Your Skills

Do not neglect the spiritual gift within you.
1 Timothy 4:14 NASB

God has blessed you with an array of talents and opportunities that are uniquely yours. Are you willing to use your gifts in the way God intends? And are you willing to summon the discipline required to develop your talents and to hone your skills? That's precisely what God wants you to do, and that's precisely what you should desire for yourself.

As you seek to expand your talents, you will undoubtedly encounter stumbling blocks along the way—things like fear of rejection or fear of failure. When you do, don't stumble! Take those concerns to God in prayer, and then keep walking in faith, refining your skills and offering your services to God. When the time is right, He will use you—but it's up to you to be thoroughly prepared when He does.

If you want to reach your potential,
you need to add a strong work ethic to your talent.
John Maxwell

Accepting God's Gifts

If your children ask for a fish, do you give them a snake instead? . . . Of course not! So if you sinful people know how to give good gifts to your children, how much more will your heavenly Father give the Holy Spirit to those who ask him.

Luke 11:11–13 NLT

God offers us priceless gifts, and it would seem silly not to accept them—yet often we don't. Why? Because we fail to trust our heavenly Father completely and because we are, at times, rather inflexible. Luke 11 teaches us that God does not withhold spiritual gifts from those who ask.

Are you asking God to move mountains in your life? Do you expect God to help you achieve the peace He has promised? Are you comfortable with the direction of your future? Whatever the size of your challenges, God is ready and willing to help you solve them. So ask for His help today, with faith and fervor, and then watch in amazement as He works in your life. Rest assured, your Father in heaven has good gifts for you.

We honor God by asking for great things when they are a part of His promise. We dishonor Him and cheat ourselves when we ask for molehills where He has promised mountains.

Vance Havner

Planning with God

Careful planning puts you ahead in the long run;
hurry and scurry puts you further behind.
Proverbs 21:5 MSG

Perhaps you have a clearly defined plan for the future. But even if you don't, rest assured that God does. Your heavenly Father has a definite plan for every aspect of your life. Your role is to sincerely seek God's guidance and to follow the guidance He gives.

Listening to God can be difficult at times because He often speaks in quieter tones than does the world around us. That's why it's so important to carve out solitary moments with Him throughout the day, prayerfully seeking His wisdom and His will.

So as you make preparations for the next stage of your life's journey, be sure to consult the ultimate Source of wisdom. When you allow God to guide your steps—when you allow His plans to become your plans—you'll be blessed indeed.

My policy has always been to ask God
to help me set goals because I believe God
has a plan for every person.
Bill Bright

The Power of Persistence

Jesus told his disciples a story to show that they should always pray and never give up.

Luke 18:1 NLT

Against the glitz of Hollywood, Katharine Hepburn's tastes tended toward men's-style shirts and khaki pants. Nominated for an incredible twelve Academy Awards, she won four. But this cinematic legend was not starstruck by her own talents—or, for that matter, the talents of others. She said, "Genius is simply the infinite capacity for taking life by the scruff of the neck."

If you'd like to make your star shine a little more brightly, don't worry about your intellect; perk up your persistence. Genius doesn't guarantee success, but persistence pays. So when you face tough times, remember Katharine Hepburn and take life fearlessly by the scruff of the neck. Because the greatest genius of all is sometimes nothing more than the genius it takes to persevere.

Don't quit. For if you do, you may miss the answer to your prayers.

Max Lucado

Unbending Truth

People with integrity walk safely,
but those who follow crooked paths will slip and fall.
Proverbs 10:9 NLT

As thoughtful adults, we know right from wrong. But we can too easily lose sight of those distinctions in a world that presents us with countless temptations dressed up in the robes of faux virtue. These temptations have the potential to harm us, in part, because they lead us to be dishonest with ourselves and with others.

Once we start bending the truth, we're likely to keep bending it. But if we acquire the habit of being completely forthright with God, with other people, and with ourselves, we'll avoid the crooked and slippery path that leads to our downfall.

The next time you're faced with an opportunity to bend the truth, choose integrity instead. When you do, your footing will remain firm and your life will be blessed.

Personal honor is the mortar that holds
the bricks of life in place.
Stephen Covey

Mistakes Happen

If we confess our sins to him, he is faithful and just to forgive us our sins and to cleanse us from all wickedness.
1 John 1:9 NLT

Accountant-turned-comedian Bob Newhart became one of America's favorite funnymen by playing bumbling characters plagued by a constant stream of blunders. But in real life, Newhart realized that the little foul-ups usually result in far less drama.

Newhart observed, "It's alright to make mistakes. The whole world isn't depending on you." That's a good reminder. Sometimes we allow little mistakes to have too big an impact on our lives.

If you're quick to beat yourself up over the little mistakes that are an inevitable part of everyday living, perhaps it's time to lighten up. You can't expect perfection from the world, and you shouldn't expect it from yourself, either. Today, do your best–and don't worry about the rest. Mistakes happen, but one of the biggest mistakes you can make is torturing yourself when they do.

If you have made mistakes, there is always another chance for you, . . . for this thing we call failure is not the falling down, but the staying down.
Mary Pickford

The Unending Source of Comfort

When doubts filled my mind, your comfort gave me renewed hope and cheer.
Psalm 94:19 NLT

Some stages of life are relatively carefree, but especially in adulthood, we all find that we must endure some difficult days . . . or even some difficult years. In times of adversity, remember the words of Jesus, who, when He walked on the waters, reassured His anxious disciples: "Take courage! It is I. Don't be afraid" (Matthew 14:27 NIV).

We, like the disciples, will have our share of doubts and fears. But because we have God's promise of eternal love and eternal life, we can face those fears with courage and with faith.

Are you facing a difficult challenge? Worried about the future? Struggling with doubt? Take courage and don't be afraid. Take your fears to God and He will replace them with hope and cheer.

When once we are assured that God is good, then there can be nothing left to fear.
Hannah Whitall Smith

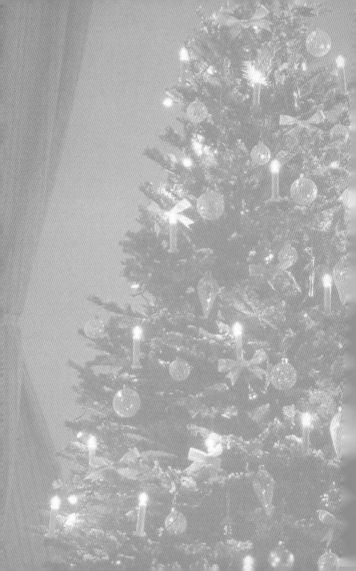

December

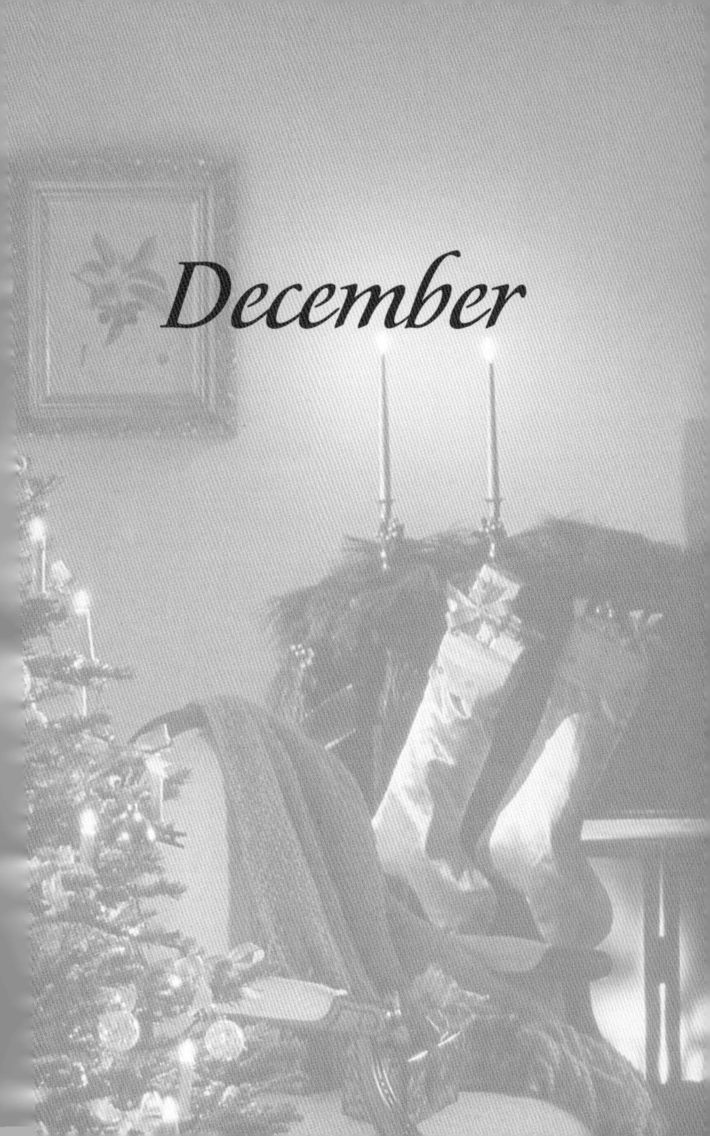

The Inner Voice

Indeed, the kingdom of God is within you.
Luke 17:21 KJV

God has given each of us a conscience: a small, quiet, inner voice that—when tuned to the frequency of His Spirit—tells us right from wrong. If we ignore that voice, we do so at our own peril. But if we obey the conscience God has placed in our hearts—if we slow down long enough to think carefully and prayerfully about the actions we're about to take—we invite God to bless us in ways we might never have dreamed possible.

Wise people make it a practice to listen carefully to that quiet internal voice. Count yourself among that number. When your conscience speaks, listen and learn. In all likelihood, God is trying to get His message through. And that's a message you need to hear.

He that loses his conscience has nothing left that is worth keeping.
Izaak Walton

Mountaintops and Valleys

I sought the Lord, and he answered me;
he delivered me from all my fears.
Psalm 34:4 NIV

Every life is an unfolding series of events–some fabulous, some not so fabulous, and some truly troubling. When you're on the mountaintops of life, praising God is easy. But when the storm clouds gather, sometimes your faith is tested, even pushed uncomfortably close to the breaking point. But when you face difficult circumstances, take comfort in this fact: wherever you are, whether at the top of the mountain or in the depths of the valley, God is there, and because He cares for you, you can live courageously.

The next time your faith and courage are stretched and strained, remember that God is on your side; He will protect you and comfort you. If you call upon Him in your hour of need, He will answer.

Courage is almost a contradiction in terms.
It means a strong desire to live taking the form
of a readiness to die.
G. K. Chesterton

Decision Making 101

An indecisive man is unstable in all his ways.
James 1:8 HCSB

When you arrive at one of life's many crossroads, here are some things you can do to help you make those important decisions:

1. Gather as much information as you can.
2. Don't be impulsive.
3. Rely on the advice of trusted friends and mentors.
4. Pray for guidance.
5. Listen to the still, small voice of the Spirit.
6. When the time for action arrives, act. Procrastination is the enemy of progress; don't let it defeat you.

People who can never quite seem to make up their minds often live in a state of discomfort. But when you sincerely seek God and line up your desires with His will, He'll help you to make the right decisions.

The Old Testament prophets did not say, "Brothers, I want a consensus."
Margaret Thatcher

When People Behave Badly

Bad temper is contagious—don't get infected.
Proverbs 22:25 MSG

Sometimes people can be unkind, even rude. When thoughtless people are unkind to you, you may be tempted to strike back, either verbally or in some other way. Don't do it! Instead, remember that God corrects other people's behaviors in His own way, and He doesn't need your help (even if you're totally convinced that He does).

So when other folks behave cruelly, foolishly, or impulsively—as they will from time to time—don't be hotheaded. Don't allow anger to hijack your emotions or your life. Instead, when someone is unkind to you, speak up for yourself as politely as you can and walk away. Forgive those folks as quickly as you can, and leave the rest up to God. When you do, the Creator will bless you with the genuine peace and comfort that are the rewards of people wise enough to forgive.

Forgiveness is not an emotion. Forgiveness is an act of the will, and the will can function regardless of the temperature of the heart.
Corrie ten Boom

Energized for Life

Be energetic in your life of salvation, reverent and sensitive before God. That energy is God's energy, an energy deep within you, God himself willing and working at what will give him the most pleasure.

Philippians 2:12–13 MSG

Are you fired with enthusiasm for life? Are you excited about your work and your calling? Are you accomplishing the most important things on your to-do list, keep finishing these tasks sooner rather than later? If so, congratulations—keep up the good work!

But if your spiritual batteries are running low, or if you can't find the strength to get everything done, then perhaps you're spending too much energy working for yourself and not enough working for God.

If you're feeling tired or troubled, don't despair. Spend a little time prioritizing your life and be sure to put first things first. Then seek strength from the Source that never fails. When you sincerely petition Him, He will give you all the strength you need to accomplish all the things you really need to do.

When the dream of our heart is one that God has planted there, a strange happiness flows into us. At that moment, all of the spiritual resources of the universe are released to help us. Our praying is then at one with the will of God and becomes a channel for the Creator's purposes for us and our world.

Catherine Marshall

If You Have Faith

Have faith in the Lord your God and you will be upheld.
2 Chronicles 20:20 NIV

Every life—including yours—is a series of successes and failures, celebrations and disappointments, joys and sorrows. Every step of the way, through every triumph and tragedy, God is with you. And He will strengthen you if you have faith in Him.

When you place your faith, your trust, indeed your life in the hands of the Creator of the universe, you'll be amazed at the marvelous things He can do with you and through you. When you trust in the Father, and when you have the support of family members and trusted friends, you'll never stay down for long.

So strengthen your faith through worship, through Bible study, and through prayer. And trust God's plans. With Him, all things are possible—and He stands ready to open a world of possibilities to you . . . if you have faith.

Faith keeps the person who keeps the faith.
Mother Teresa

Beyond Envy

Laying aside all malice, all deceit, hypocrisy, envy, and all evil speaking, as newborn babes, desire the pure milk of the word, that you may grow thereby.
1 Peter 2:1–2 NKJV

Because we are frail, imperfect human beings, one of our weaknesses is being envious of others. But God's Word warns us against envy. So if we're wise, we will guard ourselves against the natural tendency to feel a twinge of resentment or jealousy when other people experience good fortune.

Have you ever felt the pangs of envy when a friend or family member was the recipient of some good thing or experience? Have you ever been resentful when others received recognition or earned advancement? If so, here's a simple suggestion that's guaranteed to improve your attitude and lift your spirits: fill your heart with God's love, God's promises, and God's Son . . . and when you do, you'll discover that there's no room left for envy, resentment, or regret.

Never indulge in jealousy or envy. Those two destructive emotions will eat you alive.
Loretta Young

Putting Trouble Behind You

If you do nothing in a difficult time,
your strength is limited.
Proverbs 24:10 HCSB

William James was the son of a noted theologian, the brother of a great novelist, a Harvard professor, and one of the founding fathers of American psychology. He was also a common-sense philosopher who once observed, "Nothing is so fatiguing as the eternal hanging on of an uncompleted task." How true.

Sometimes it's tempting to postpone the unpleasant, thus allowing minor problems to mushroom. But as James was quick to point out, procrastination is sand in the machinery of life. So do yourself a favor: finish the unfinished work (even it's unpleasant) before you begin something else. Because the very best place to put trouble is behind you.

All that is necessary to break the spell of inertia and frustration is this: act as if it were impossible to fail. That is . . . the command of right about face which turns us from failure to success.
Dorothea Brande

The Joys of Friendship

I thank my God every time I remember you.
Philippians 1:3 NIV

What is a friend? One dictionary defines the word *friend* as "a person who is attached to another by feelings of affection or personal regard." This definition is accurate, as far as it goes; however, when we examine the deeper meaning of friendship, so many more descriptors come to mind: trustworthiness, loyalty, helpfulness, kindness, encouragement, humor, and cheerfulness, to mention but a few.

Today, as you consider the many blessings God has entrusted to your care, remember to thank Him for the friends He has chosen to place along your path. Thank your heavenly Father for the comfort and joy your friends add to your life. And promise yourself that you'll be a source of encouragement to them, just as they are to you.

The only way to have a friend is to be one.
Ralph Waldo Emerson

Letting Go of the Past

You're familiar with the command to the ancients, "Do not murder." I'm telling you that anyone who is so much as angry with a brother or sister is guilty of murder.

Matthew 5:21–22 MSG

Do you invest more time than you should reliving the past or dreaming of revenge? Are you troubled by feelings of anger, bitterness, or regret? If so, it's time to get serious about putting the past in its proper place—behind you.

Perhaps there's something in your past that you deeply regret. Or maybe you've been scarred by a trauma you simply can't seem to get over. Why not make today the day you ask for God's help—sincerely and prayerfully—as you determine, once and for all, to move beyond yesterday's pain so you can fully savor the precious present.

Of course, it's natural to want to lick the wounds of injustices you've suffered and to hold grudges against the people who inflicted them. But God has a better plan: He wants you to live in the present, not the past because He knows you'll be happier and healthier when you do.

Don't waste today's time cluttering up tomorrow's opportunities with yesterday's troubles.

Barbara Johnson

Directing Your Thoughts

People's thoughts can be like a deep well,
but someone with understanding
can find the wisdom there.
Proverbs 20:5 NCV

Paul Valéry said, "We hope vaguely but dread precisely." How true. All too often we allow our worries to dominate our thoughts and cloud our vision. What we need is renewed faith, clearer perspective, and a fresh focus.

When we focus on the frustrations of today or the uncertainties of tomorrow, we rob ourselves of peace in the present moment. But when we direct our thoughts in more positive paths, we rob our worries of the power to tyrannize us.

Today, remember that God is infinitely greater than the challenges you face. Remember also that your thoughts have a powerful affect on your sense of well-being, so guard–and direct–them accordingly.

Human thoughts have a tendency to turn themselves into their physical equivalents.
Earl Nightingale

God's Love for You

He who does not love does not know God, for God is love.
1 John 4:8 NKJV

God loves you. He loves you more than you can imagine, and His affection is deeper than you can fathom. And as a result of His love, you have an important decision to make. You must decide what to do about God's love: you can return it . . . or reject it.

When you accept the love that flows from the heart of God, it will transform you. When you embrace God's love, you'll feel different about yourself, your neighbors, your community, your church, and your world. When you open your heart to God's love, you will feel compelled to share God's message–and His compassion–with others. God's heart is overflowing with love for you. Accept it, return it, and share it with someone today.

God loves you, and He yearns for you to turn away from the path of evil. You need His forgiveness, and you need Him to come into your life and remake you from within.
Billy Graham

The God Who Heals

He heals the brokenhearted and bandages their wounds.
Psalm 147:3 NCV

When we suffer heartbreak, it may seem, at least to us, that our hearts can never be repaired. But God knows better. He knows that we can recover, and He promises that when we ask for His help, He will answer our prayers (Luke 11:9–10).

Has your heart been broken? Are you feeling troubled, confused, weak, or sorrowful? If so, please remember that God is not just near; He is right here, right now, trying to get His message of love through to you. So open your heart to the Creator; spend quiet time with Him today (and every day); ask Him to comfort your spirit, heal your heart, and ease your mind. Don't expect healing to be instantaneous, but do expect it to come in time . . . just as God has promised.

A mighty fortress is our God,
a bulwark never failing our helper He,
amid the flood of mortal ills prevailing.
Martin Luther

Focusing on the Future

One thing I do, forgetting those things which are behind and reaching forward to those things which are ahead, I press toward the goal for the prize of the upward call of God in Christ Jesus.

Philippians 3:13–14 NKJV

During his thirteen-year tenure at Notre Dame, Knute Rockne gained a permanent and prominent place in football history. His teams enjoyed five undefeated seasons and featured such stars as the "Four Horsemen" and the legendary George Gipp. Rockne advised, "The past is history. Make the present good, and the past will take care of itself." The coach understood that it's tempting to focus on what might have been—tempting, but unproductive.

So if you're looking for a sure-fire way to improve your tomorrows, let go of yesterday and take firm hold of today. Because you can't change the past, but you can change the future, one day at a time. And today is the best day to start.

If we open a quarrel between past and present, we shall find that we have lost the future.

Winston Churchill

Happiness and Holiness

Happy are the people who live at your Temple. . . .
Happy are those whose strength comes from you.
Psalm 84:4–5 NCV

Do you seek happiness, abundance, and contentment? If so, here are some things you should do: love God; depend on Him for strength; try, to the best of your abilities, to follow His will; and strive to obey His instructions. When you do these things, you'll discover that happiness goes hand in hand with holiness.

The happiest people are not those who struggle against God's will, insisting on their own way; the happiest folks are those who walk with God and trust His guidance.

True happiness is always available—and you need not wait until tomorrow to claim it. So today, focus less on your obstacles and more on God's gifts. Strive, as best you can, to be a genuinely holy person and leave the rest up to God. Then prepare yourself for the blessings—and joys—that are sure to follow.

To be in a state of true grace is to be miserable no more; it is to be happy forever.
A soul in this state is a soul near and dear to God.
It is a soul housed in God.
Thomas Brooks

When We Are Weak, He Is Strong

The God of all grace, who called you to His eternal glory in Christ Jesus, will personally restore, establish, strengthen, and support you.

1 Peter 5:10 HCSB

The line from the children's song is both familiar and comforting: "Little ones to Him belong. We are weak, but He is strong." And it's a message that applies to kids of all ages: we are all, at times, weak but we worship a mighty God who meets our needs and answers our prayers.

Today, as you encounter the inevitable challenges of daily living, you can turn to God for strength. After all, God's Word promises that you can do all things through Him (Philippians 4:13). The challenge, then, is clear: to place God where He belongs, at the very center of your life. When you do, you will discover that, yes, God loves you and, yes, He will give you the direction and strength you need. Ask Him to help you today.

The Lord is the one who travels every mile of the wilderness way as our leader, cheering us, supporting and supplying and fortifying us.

Elisabeth Elliot

The Attitude of a Leader

*Those who are wise will shine like the brightness
of the heavens, and those who lead many to righteousness,
like the stars for ever and ever.*

Daniel 12:3 NIV

John Maxwell wrote, "Great leaders understand that the right attitude will set the right atmosphere, which enables the right response from others." If you are in a position of leadership, whether as a parent or as a leader at your workplace, your church, or your school, you can set the right tone by maintaining the right attitude.

Our world needs effective leadership and part of that world is made up of your family members and coworkers. You can become a trusted, competent, thoughtful leader if you learn to maintain the right attitude–one that's realistic, optimistic, and forward looking. When you do these things, you'll be the kind of leader that others will want to follow.

*What I need is someone who will
make me do what I can.*

Ralph Waldo Emerson

On a Mission for God

You are a chosen people. You are royal priests,
a holy nation, God's very own possession. As a result,
you can show others the goodness of God, for he called
you out of the darkness into his wonderful light.

1 Peter 2:9 NLT

Whether you realize it or not, you are on a personal mission for God. That mission is straightforward: honor God, follow Him, and serve His children.

Of course, you will encounter obstacles as you attempt to discover the exact nature of God's purpose for your life. You must never lose sight of the overriding purposes God has established for all people—that we worship Him sincerely and that we love our neighbors as we love ourselves.

Every day presents opportunities for you to honor God with your words, your prayers, and your service. When you do, you will be blessed in amazing ways. So today, seek God's will, serve His children, trust His promises, and enjoy His bountiful rewards.

Without God, life has no purpose,
and without purpose, life has no meaning.

Rick Warren

Glorious Opportunities

Make the most of every opportunity.
Colossians 4:5 NIV

Are you excited about the opportunities of today and thrilled by the possibilities of tomorrow? Do you confidently expect God to lead you to a place of fulfillment, peace, and joy? Do you expect to receive the priceless gift of eternal life when your days on earth are over? If you trust God's promises, then you can trust that your future is intensely and eternally bright.

Today, as you prepare to meet the challenges and fulfill the duties of the day, pause for a moment and meditate on God's promises. Think about the wonderful future He has in store for you. God has promised that when you walk with Him, your future is secure. Trust that promise and celebrate it. Then step out in faith and seize the day, making the most of every opportunity it presents. Praise God for His gifts . . . and use them in ways that will make Him proud.

You don't just luck into things . . . ;
You build step by step,
whether it is friendships or opportunities.
Barbara Bush

The Chains of Perfectionism

Those who wait for perfect weather will never plant seeds; those who look at every cloud will never harvest crops.

Ecclesiastes 11:4 NCV

There's never a "perfect" time to do anything. That's why we can always find reasons to put off until tomorrow the things we should be doing today.

If you find yourself bound by the chains of perfectionism and procrastination, ask yourself what you're waiting for or, more accurately, what you're afraid of and why. As you examine the emotional roadblocks that have, heretofore, blocked your path, you may discover that you're waiting for the "perfect" moment, that instant when you feel neither afraid nor anxious. But in truth, perfect moments like these are few and far between.

So stop waiting for the perfect moment and focus, instead, on finding the right moment to do what needs to be done. Then trust God and step out in faith. When you do, you'll discover that with God's help, you can accomplish great things . . . and that you can accomplish them sooner rather than later.

Better to do something imperfectly than to do nothing flawlessly.

Robert Schuller

God-Prompted Priorities

Seek first God's kingdom and what God wants.
Then all your other needs will be met as well.
Matthew 6:33 NCV

Have you asked God to help prioritize your life? Have you asked Him for guidance and for the courage to do the things you know need to be done? If you do, then you'll not only be keeping your checklist in check but also inviting God to reveal Himself in various ways as you go about your day.

When you make God a full partner in every aspect of your life, He will lead you along the proper path—His path. When you allow God to reign in your heart, He will shower you with spiritual blessings that are too numerous to count and too amazing to anticipate. So as you plan for the day ahead, let God prompt your priorities. It's the surest way to have everything you need to get through your day . . . and your life.

The moment you wake up each morning, all your wishes and hopes for the day rush at you like wild animals. And the first job each morning consists in shoving it all back; in listening to that other voice, taking that other point of view, letting that other, larger, stronger, quieter life coming flowing in.

C. S. Lewis

The Greatest Among Us

Whoever wants to become great among you must be your servant, and whoever wants to be first among you must be your slave; just as the Son of Man did not come to be served, but to serve, and to give His life—a ransom for many.

Matthew 20:26–28 HCSB

Jesus taught that the most esteemed men and women are not the leaders of society or the captains of industry. To the contrary, the Son of God said that the greatest among us are those who choose to minister and to serve.

Today, you may feel the temptation to build yourself up in the eyes of those you encounter. But if you want to be great in God's estimation, choose, instead, to serve your neighbors quietly and without fanfare. Be generous, compassionate, and, perhaps, even anonymous. Then, when you have done your best to serve your community and to serve your Creator, you can rest comfortably knowing that in the eyes of God, you have achieved greatness. After all, God's eyes are the ones that really count.

Service is the pathway to real significance.

Rick Warren

Accepting the Past

Shall I not drink from the cup of suffering
the Father has given me?
John 18:11 NLT

Has disappointment or tragedy left you feeling embittered toward God and angry at the world? If so, let today be the day you find the strength to accept the unchangeable past—and the comfort of faith in the promise of tomorrow. It's time to trust God completely and to reclaim the peace—His peace—that can and should be yours.

When you encounter situations you don't understand, remember that God does understand and has a reason for everything He does. God doesn't often explain His actions in ways that we, as mortals with limited insight, can comprehend. So instead of demanding understanding in every aspect of God's unfolding plan for our lives and our world, we must be satisfied to trust Him. But that's part of the plan—to develop our faith. We may not know God's plan or understand His actions. But we can trust Him to make everything, even our troubled past and trying present, work together for good.

Acceptance says: True, this is my situation at the moment. I'll look unblinkingly at the reality of it. But I'll also open my hands to accept willingly whatever a loving Father sends me.

Catherine Marshall

In Times of Adversity

Whatever is born of God overcomes the world.
And this is the victory
that has overcome the world—our faith.
1 John 5:4 NKJV

All of us face times of adversity. On occasion, we must endure the disappointments and tragedies that befall believers and nonbelievers alike. But the reassuring words of 1 John 5:4 remind us that when we accept God's grace, we will be able to overcome the passing hardships of this world by relying on His strength, His love, and His promise of eternal life.

When we call upon God in heartfelt prayer, He will answer—in His own time and according to His own plan. He will comfort us in our distress. And while we're waiting for God's plan to unfold and for His healing touch to restore us, we can rest in the knowledge that our Creator can overcome any obstacle, even if we cannot. Today, take courage; when you take God at His word and trust Him, your faith will overcome your adversity.

Pain is the fuel of passion—
it energizes us with an intensity to change
that we don't normally possess.
Rick Warren

Faith, Not Fear

In the multitude of my anxieties within me,
Your comforts delight my soul.
Psalm 94:19 NKJV

God can give us the power to live above and beyond our anxieties. Our heavenly Father wants us to live by faith, not by fear. He instructs us to trust Him completely, this day and forever. But sometimes trusting God feels difficult, especially when we become caught up in the incessant anxieties of a worried world.

When you feel anxious—and you will—turn your thoughts to God's love. When you're worried or weak, turn your concerns over to Him. Then you can take comfort in the knowledge that no problems (including yours) are too big for God.

Today, take your concerns to the Creator in prayer, and to the best of your ability, leave them there. Let His comfort delight your soul.

Worry and anxiety are sand in the machinery of life; faith is the oil.
E. Stanley Jones

The Balancing Act

Grow a wise heart—you'll do yourself a favor;
keep a clear head—you'll find a good life.
Proverbs 19:8 MSG

Life is a delicate balancing act, a tightrope walk with overcommitment on one side and undercommitment on the other. And it's up to each of us to walk carefully on that rope, not falling prey to pride (which causes us to attempt too much) or to fear (which causes us to attempt too little).

God's Word promises us the possibility of spiritual abundance. And we are far more likely to experience that abundance when we lead balanced lives.

Are you doing too much—or too little? If so, maybe it's time to have a little chat with God. If you listen carefully to His instructions, He'll help you achieve a more balanced life—a life that's right for you and your loved ones. And when you strike the right balance in life, everybody wins.

To do too much is as dangerous as to do nothing at all.
Both modes prevent us from savoring our moments. One
causes me to rush right past
the best of life without recognizing or basking in it, and
the other finds me sitting quietly
as life rushes past me.
Patsy Clairmont

Beyond Bitterness

Don't insist on getting even; that's not for you to do. "I'll do the judging," says God. "I'll take care of it."
Romans 12:19 MSG

Bitterness is a spiritual sickness. It will consume your soul; it is dangerous to your emotional health. It can destroy you if you let it . . . so don't let it!

If you're caught up in feelings of anger or resentment, you know all too well the destructive power of those emotions. How can you rid yourself of these feelings? First, prayerfully ask God to cleanse your heart. Then, learn to catch yourself whenever thoughts of bitterness or hatred seep into your mind. Learn to resist those negative thoughts before they hijack your emotions.

The Bible teaches us that if we judge our brothers and sisters, we, too, will be judged . . . by God. Let us refrain, then, from judging our neighbors. Instead, let us forgive them and love them, while leaving their judgment to a far more capable Authority. Our hearts will be much lighter when we do.

By not forgiving, by not letting wrongs go, we aren't getting back at anyone. We are merely punishing ourselves by barricading our own hearts.
Jim Cymbala

The Guidebook

The word of the Lord endures forever. And this is the word that was preached as the gospel to you.

1 Peter 1:25 HCSB

God has given us a guidebook for righteous living: It's called the Bible. This book contains thorough instructions that, if followed, lead to fulfillment, righteousness, and eternal life. But if we choose to ignore God's commandments, we tragically forfeit those rewards.

God has given us the Bible not to smother us in rules, as some suggest, but so that we can know His promises, His power, His wisdom, His love, and His Son. As we study God's teachings and apply them to our lives, we live by the Word that will never pass away. When we walk with God that way, it's not a burden; it's a joy.

Today, make God's book the guide for your life. Ask Him to help you follow His instructions and to live in such a way that you'll be a shining example to your family, friends, and, most importantly, to those who don't yet know Him.

The Bible was not given to increase our knowledge but to change our lives.

D. L. Moody

A Series of Choices

I am offering you life or death, blessings or curses. Now, choose life! . . . To choose life is to love the Lord your God, obey him, and stay close to him.

Deuteronomy 30:19–20 NCV

Life is a series of choices. And as a thoughtful person who has been richly blessed by the Creator, you have every reason, and every tool you need, to make wise choices. But sometimes, when the daily grind threatens to grind you up and spit you out, it can seem more convenient to make unwise choices—even choices that are displeasing to God. If you do, you'll forfeit the happiness and comfort that might otherwise have been yours.

So today, as you make the many choices your path presents, ask God to help you choose wisely. When you choose to love God and stay close to Him, he promises life and blessings in return.

I believe with all my heart and soul that at every important crossroads in my life I was faced with a choice: between right and wrong, between serving God and pleasing myself. I didn't always make the right choice. In fact, I stumbled down the wrong path more times than I marched down the right one. But God heard the earnest prayers of those who loved me and by His grace brought me to my knees.

Al Green

Learning to Stay True to Yourself

There's something here also for seasoned men and women, still a thing or two for the experienced to learn.
Proverbs 1:5–6 MSG

Leonard Slye was born in the big city of Cincinnati, Ohio, but he moved west, changed his name to Roy Rogers, and became one of America's favorite singing cowboys. Rogers was the only man ever elected to the Country Music Hall of Fame twice—first as a founding member of the band The Sons of the Pioneers and then as a solo artist. His classic theme song, "Happy Trails," was written by his wife and costar Dale Evans.

Rogers' friend and fellow singer Randy Travis observed, "In real life, he was exactly like he was in the movies. He really was Roy Rogers all the time." In other words, Roy was a straight shooter.

Whether you're a cowboy, a cowgirl, or a city slicker, you can take a tip from Roy and be a genuine article. Learn to stay true to yourself. When you do, it's happy trails to you.

Life is a journey; every experience is here to teach you more fully how to be who you really are.
Oprah Winfrey

Courage for the Journey

Since God assured us, "I'll never let you down, never walk off and leave you," we can boldly quote, God is there, ready to help; I'm fearless no matter what.

Hebrews 13:5–6 MSG

As you take the next step in your life's journey, are you willing to enlist God as your traveling companion? Are you willing to trust Him, to obey Him, to honor Him, and to love Him? Are you willing to consult Him before you make important decisions, not just run to Him after things don't go well? If you can answer these questions with a resounding yes, you will know great peace and comfort all of your days.

Today, as a gift to yourself and your loved ones, summon the courage to follow God. Even if the path seems difficult, even if your heart is fearful, trust your heavenly Father and follow Him. Trust Him with your day and with your life. Do His work, care for His children, and share His good news. Let Him guide your steps. He will never leave you, and He will never lead you astray.

Trusting God completely means having faith that He knows what is best for your life. You expect Him to keep His promises, help you with problems, and do the impossible when necessary.

Rick Warren

Notes

These pages have been provided
for your personal journaling and meditation.

Notes

Notes

Notes

Notes

Notes

Notes

Notes

Scripture References

Scripture quotations marked CEV are taken from the Contemporary English Version, copyright © 1995 by American Bible Society. Used by permission.

Scripture quotations marked HCSB are taken from the Holman Christian Standard Bible®, copyright © 1999, 2000, 2002, 2003 by Holman Bible Publishers. Used by permission.

Scripture quotations marked KJV are taken from the Holy Bible, King James Version.

Scripture quotations marked MSG are taken from The Message, copyright © 1993, 1994, 1995, 1996, 2000, 2001, 2002. Used by permission of NavPress Publishing Group.

Scripture quotations marked NASB are taken from the New American Standard Bible, copyright © 1960, 1962, 1963, 1968, 1971, 1972, 1973, 1975, 1977, 1995 by The Lockman Foundation. Used by permission.

Scripture quotations marked NCV are taken from the Holy Bible, New Century Version®, copyright © 1987, 1988, 1991, 2005 by Thomas Nelson, Inc. Used by permission. All rights reserved.

Scripture quotations marked NIV are taken from the Holy Bible, New International Version ®, copyright © 1973, 1978, 1984 by International Bible Society. Used by permission of Zondervan Publishing House. All rights reserved.

Scripture quotations marked NKJV are taken from the Holy Bible, New King James Version, copyright © 1982, 1988 by Thomas Nelson, Inc. All rights reserved.

Scripture quotations marked NLT are taken from the Holy Bible, New Living Translation, copyright © 1996, 2004 by Tyndale Charitable Trust. Used by permission of Tyndale House Publishers, Inc., Carol Stream, Illinois 60188. All rights reserved.

Scripture quotations marked TLB are taken from The Living Bible, copyright © 1971 owned by assignment by KNT Charitable Trust. Used by permission of Tyndale House Publishers, Inc., Carol Stream, Illinois 60188. All rights reserved.

Scripture quotations marked TNIV are taken from the Holy Bible, Today's New International Version®, copyright © 2001, 2005 by International Bible Society®. Used by permission of International Bible Society®. All rights reserved worldwide.

Also available in the Hugs Daily Inspirations series . . .

Hugs Daily Inspirations for Women
Hugs Daily Inspirations, Words of Promise
Hugs Daily Inspirations for Moms

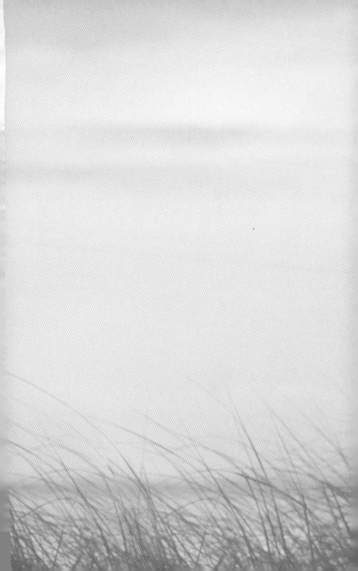